Seven Decades of Student Driven Publishing

Humboldt State University

© 2021 Humboldt State University

The work is made available under a Creative Commons Attribution-Non-commercial CC BY-NC License

Reproduction, posting, transmission, or other distribution of use of the work beyond the permission granted by the Creative Commons license requires written agreement by the current Humboldt State University Toyon Literary Magazine faculty advisor.

Toyon Literary Magazine
Founders Hall 205
Humboldt State University
1 Harpst Street
Arcata, California 95521-8299
toyonliterarymagazine@gmail.com

Book and Cover Design: Sarah Godlin
Cover Illustration: "Raven" by Elisa N. Griego
Authors: Erika Andrews, Asha Galindo

Humboldt State University Press
ISBN: 978-1-947112-54-4

Contents

How to Use this Book	vii
Acknowledgments	ix
The 1950s	1
The 1960s	9
The 1970s	21
The 1980s	29
The 1990s	43
The 2000s	53
The 2010s	65
The 2020s	83
Making Toyon	87
Notes from the Authors	96
People of Toyon	101

How to Use this Book

Toyon: Seven Decades of Student Driven Publishing is meant to capture the history and spirit of Toyon literary journal from its origin in 1954 to the future that surely will exist beyond these pages. The aim of this book is to inform future Toyon staffers of the unique history of the publication, to stress the importance of maintaining archives, and to provide insight into the inner workings of book/magazine production over the last 60+ years.

This book is also a place to tell the story of a student-run publication from the perspective of the student. We are two former *Toyon* staff members who worked on issues 65 and 66, in the years of 2019 and 2020, respectively. We hope that these pages will entertain as well as educate—and that it truly honors the passionate and dynamic voices of the student editors, contributors, and volunteers that have published this magazine year after year.

We have strived to include many details and first-hand accounts and to properly interpret the information archived in the Humboldt State University library special collections. As with any archive, gaps remain in the history of *Toyon* that we've been able to access; for some periods we had very little information other than the finished magazine. In these instances, we worked hard to summarize what we could and fill in gaps using course catalogues and other materials from the archives to properly capture the era.

People of Toyon:

Toyon thrives off of the people and personalities who have made the journal what it is over the years. Throughout the book we have highlighted several key players. We finish these highlights with a complete list of *Toyon* mastheads: staff, editors, and advisors from 1954-present. We are all people of *Toyon* really.

Toyon Lore:

These are the legends of *Toyon*, the stories, the rumors, the mysteries, and the special magic of students creating and publishing for themselves, often for the first time.

Acknowledgments

This book project was funded by the generous support of the Humboldt State University Emeritus and Retired Faculty Association (ERFA). The authors, the staff members of *Toyon*, and faculty advisor Janelle Adsit extend heartfelt thanks to the members of ERFA for their encouragement of *Toyon* and this project. We wish to also thank the HSU Library, HSU Special Collections, and HSU Press—especially Kyle Morgan, Carly Marino, and Louis Knecht—for guiding the research and publication process. Thanks also to the HSU English Department and the HSU College of Arts, Humanities, and Social Sciences for their sustaining support. Deep thanks also go to Sarah Godlin, who designed the book and stepped onto this project with a short timeline. Thanks to Sarah for all she has contributed to *Toyon* over the years as a staff member and as someone who continues to educate the student staff. Thanks also go to Marcos Hernandez, who serves as the administrator and current faculty advisor for *Toyon*.

The research for this book builds on several years of research by *Toyon* Archive Editors including Jade Mejia, AJ McGough, Drew Ahlberg, and Korinza Shlanta; we wish to express thanks for these editors' work in curating the *Toyon* archives and digitizing the back issues on the *Toyon* website. During the English 460 course students are asked to research and write about people and events from *Toyon*'s history. Some of the work from these projects have been re-purposed in this book and we would like to acknowledge the time and effort students contributed to preserving this history.

Special note to the editors of *Toyon*:

We would like to encourage current and future staff members to please archive materials used to make *Toyon* each year. Even the small things like logo designs and grandiose wish lists for the future are important artifacts to add to the existing *Toyon* archives. The exchange of first-hand information about your role on *Toyon* is one of the best ways to preserve our *Toyon* history; remember, you're writing that history. We encourage future managing editors and assistant managers to always write an editor's note to tell a story about each volume, and we recommend that the entire staff will express themselves via staff biographies. Remember that no one can tell these stories but You.

The 1950s

1954
- April 9, 1954: The first volume of *Toyon* was published.
- The English Department didn't officially support *Toyon* or publish it through the department, but two of the department's professors at the time, Dr. Reginald White and Dr. Giles Sinclair, are credited as the "real editors and the final arbiters."
- Fall 1954: Toyon was officially supported and published through the English Department.
- Librarian Charles Bloom published a poem in this volume titled "Upon Buenos Aires"

1955
- *Toyon* did not publish this year.
- The Vietnam War was officially declared on November 1, 1956.

1956
- According to the staff letter, *Toyon* published only works that were turned in to the staff with no particular viewpoint they were trying to push. A good amount of the pieces in this volume revolved around war and ideas of democracy.

1957
- This volume was printed on "Safety Orange" paper and was sold for 25 cents
- All contributors were allotted a short bio about themselves. This was the first appearance of bios for authors.

1958
- This was the first volume published like an actual book; others were broadsheet style.
- This was the first and only volume to offer Screenwriting as a genre

1959
- Lucky Logger is adopted as the mascot for Humboldt State College.

The Fifties: The Beginning

The 1950s are often idealized as a time of prosperity following decades of depression and war. The heteronormative nuclear family, anchored by a father figure and a stay-at-home mother, were central to the picture of perfection. However, while the enduring image of the 1950s is one of suburban white picket fences, the writing that was published in early *Toyon* issues challenges the picturesque happiness.

The 1950s also saw the setting of The Korean War, which the U.S. was embroiled in, as well as the Vietnam War, which affected the publication of *Toyon* and influenced the contents of volume 3. According to the staff letter, *Toyon* published only works that were turned into the staff with no particular viewpoint or agenda on the part of the writer. A good amount of the pieces in this volume revolved around war and ideas of democracy. While it seems the students were cognizant of the controversial nature of war, they also made an effort to remain neutral as editors. This

First Volume, 1954

Volume 2, 1956

could be seen as a sign of journalistic integrity on the part of editors, or conversely a sign of the times where it was more important to give the impression of impartiality.

Still, students found ways to express their opinions, like a satirical critique of the deer-hunters in the 1950s, titled " A Modest Proposal after Jonathan Swift" by Pat Hammond, published in the inaugural volume. It is a direct response to 17th Century Irish author and satirist Jonathan Swift's piece "A Modest Proposal" in which he suggests that the Irish eat their children in order to prevent them from suffering under English hegemony. Hammond's piece suggests that deer-hunters should be hunted like game and displayed as such in order to "help us rid the state of one of its most destructive pests." The push back against a stuffy literary establishment in this piece and several more published in the early years of *Toyon* set the tone for future editors and contributors. The true spirit of *Toyon* was born!

Volume 3, 1957   **Volume 4, 1958**   **Volume 5, 1959**

People of Toyon

Favorite Librarian: Charles Bloom

Toyon magazine was named by librarian, nature enthusiast, photographer, and beloved mentor, Charles Bloom. After coming to HSU in 1952, he quickly became an active member of the community. He suggested the name *Toyon* for the just-beginning, student-produced creative arts journal. Although the journal itself has undergone many transformations, Bloom's influence lasts in the simple and symbolic title that connects the magazine to the local terrain and flora. He even had a piece published in an early edition of the *Toyon*; called "Upon Buenos Aires," the piece consisted of a series of journal entries—an early example of the legacy of creative nonfiction work in *Toyon*.

When he wasn't working as a research librarian, Bloom was hiking, fishing, and taking pictures of the incredible landscapes of Humboldt County. Upon his death in May of 1998, he donated his collection of photographs spanning four consecutive decades to the Special Collections room of the library in which he devoted his life to the students of HSU. His photos show pristine and beautiful mountains, forests, and rivers along with life at HSU and pictures of surrounding towns. Charles Bloom also led the hiking group on campus, known as Boots 'n Blisters, whose members hiked for three decades. His other accomplishments include the publication of his library guide, *Ways to the Wildeness:* a list of books on wilderness travel in the Library, California State University, Humboldt.

He was crowned the winner of the "Ugliest Professor Contest" at the annual Lumberjack Days campus celebration.

A man on the move, Bloom often explored new horizons each year, and he wrote a nature poem annually to send out to fellow librarians as a Christmas newsletter. His poems centered around his travels, nature, and the coming of the holiday season. Often funny and sentimental, he commiserates in one poem about the long rainy season Humboldt students know so well:

```
     "And as the weary weeks go by
         All clammy, cold, and gray,
   Good Humboldt folks, well dampened down,
          Grow moldier by the day;"
       -(Charles Bloom, 1986: Something Fishy)
       Charles Bloom, HSU Library Nov. 1952
```

He was well-loved by his students and colleges and kept regular correspondence with fellow librarian, Dean Galloway who described Bloom's letters saying "the joy, of course, comes from the bits of news couched in Bloomer style." He retired from his work in the library in 1983, but his influence on the *Toyon Literary Magazine*, in name and in its connection to the natural world, continues on.

—Gloria Pearlman, previously published on toyonlitewrarymagazine.org

Citations: Bloom, Charles. HSU Library, Staff File. Arcata, 1952-1983. Bloom, Charles. Charles Bloom Slide Collection. Arcata, 1952. Galloway, Dean. Received by Charles Bloom, Iran, 8 Feb. 1957, Tehran.

TOYON LORE

In Defense of the Bushes

The first thing most people ask about *Toyon* is, well, "what's a toyon?" And why would our esteemed literary journal be named after it? Truthfully, it isn't much of a story. A toyon is a California native bush that can be found on the HSU campus, and throughout the state. It's also known as a California holly berry. It's the kind of plant that you've most likely seen in front yards and in shopping malls but never had a name for. It's not particularly special, it's flowers are too small to add to floral arrangements, and its berries are not commonly eaten by humans, although they are enjoyed by birds.

That is kind of where the early editors' heads were at. It was actually librarian Charles Bloom who had the idea to call it *Toyon*. Beverly Dahlen and other founding students agreed because they thought it sounded musical and besides, this project was "for the birds," anyway.

Toyon Berries

Different students have had various ways of expressing the *Toyon*. The bush has been depicted in art on the cover and in logos. A recent suggestion was for a toyon bush mascot, similar to Lucky the Lumberjack—but this one is plant shaped and wants to expand your literary horizons!

If we break down the characteristics of the toyon shrub you can determine how it qualifies as a worthy muse for a literary journal. Toyon grows all over California's coasts and in the Sierra foothills, just like many of our students. Its vibrant berries once covered the hills of Southern California and were once believed to be the inspiration for the naming of Hollywood. While that's not quite the truth, toyon berries are still eye-catching and striking almost like the art and writing that grows from the students of the university. Though the berries contain small amounts of cyanide, this can be lightly cooked out, suggesting that the pieces in *Toyon* must be read deeper to extract the good stuff. It's evergreen with sharpened leaves, naive but tough. Modern students will love that toyon is one of the few plants that has kept its common Native American name, given by the Ohlone people of the California coast (though this probably wasn't a criterion when the magazine was titled). Most of all, toyon is drought adapted and can be fire retardant when given enough water, which just means it grows very well, very quickly in the dry and warm areas of California, and that is just good information to take with you as a friend to the environment. If you're a reader, contributor, or staffer of *Toyon*, the magazine, you already are a friend.

The 1960s

SPRING - 1963

1960
- First issue to include a contest and prize: the "Dorothy Fish Kerr Poetry Contest."

1961
- Raymond Carver published for the first time in Spring '61.

1962
- Two issues were published this year in January (volume 8) and May (volume 9).

1963
- Volume 10 is known as the infamous "Carver Coup" issue.

1964
- Volume 11's statement of intent shifts the focus away from simply presenting student works to "[provide] the challenge of publication and develop...a sense of responsibility to an audience." This demarcated one of the first of many transitions in how publishing, writing, art, and the meaning of what *Toyon* is for students of Humboldt State University.

1965
- Jim Dodge published in the journal as an undergraduate, not yet advisor of *Toyon*.

1966
- The "Anonymous, none" of 1966: Within the pages of the 19th volume of Toyon, published in 1966, are three peculiar poems archived as "Anonymous, none." While "Anonymous" signifies the name of the author, or lack thereof, "none" denotes the title of the entry. All the "Anonymous, none" poems wrestle with dark emotionality and unpack traumatic events. It is understandable wanting to publish pieces that are touchier in subject anonymously, but why not title them? With such rawness and anonymity of each piece, it calls to mind a famous quote by Virginia Woolf who states: "for most of history, Anonymous was a woman." Could these writers be women or part of another marginalized group who just wanted their story to be told without fear of repercussion? It is hard to say. All of us at *Toyon* appreciate the boldness of these writers, while we do not accept Anonymous submission anymore, pen names are welcome. The "Anonymous, none" might be untraceable in name, but their words live forever in our history.

1969
- Only issue of Toyon to never be distributed because of nudity.

-Additional timeline research by Korinza Shlanta and Theressa Lopez

The Sixties: Leading the Charge

The 60s was the first full decade of *Toyon*. It was also a time of experimentation for the students of Humboldt State College (as it was called in the 1960s). The world around the college was changing: in 1963 President John F. Kennedy was assassinated; winter 1964 brought the 'Thousand Year Flood' to Humboldt and Del Norte counties that isolated the campus; and first lady Lady Bird Johnson dedicated Redwood National Park in 1968. The campus itself was growing from just over 2,000 students enrolled in 1960 to 5,100 in 1969. The library and Sequoia theatre (now Van Duzen Theatre) were built along with eight new dormitories that were co-ed by the end of the decade.

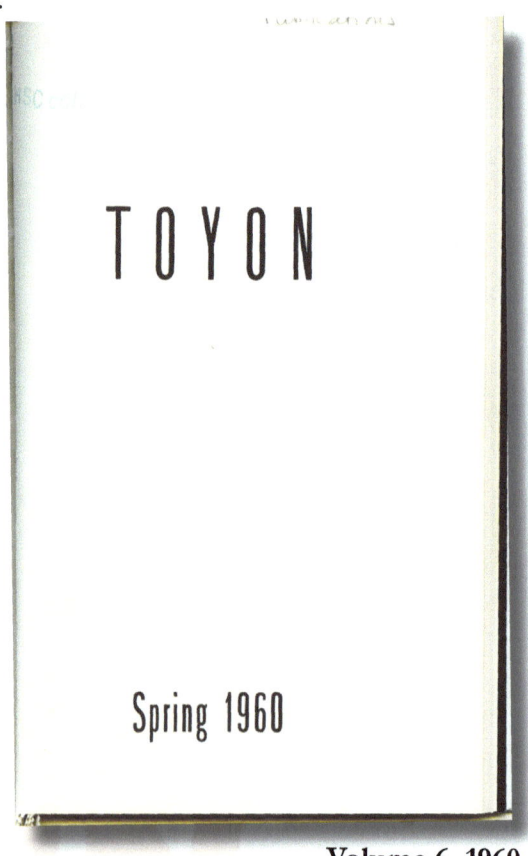

Volume 6, 1960

Amidst the changing social landscape of the world, Humboldt State was a relatively conservative campus. According to Steven Phipps, one of the editors of the 1969 edition, the school and *Toyon* had been "stodgy," meaning uninspired. Early issues of the 60s show evidence of that: there is very little art and no photography. The nameplate on the 1962 "newsprint" issues takes itself seriously, stating that "*Toyon* exists to encourage students of Humboldt State College to take an interest in original literary composition." But as the 60s wore on, the student editors pushed boundaries and took risks.

1960s

The 1963 edition of the book editor was none other than Raymond Carver, a well-known writer who revitalized the short story in the 1980s. In 1963, he was an undergraduate at Humboldt State and was beginning to hone his signature minimalist style. Anecdotal stories of the "Carver Coup" claim he wrote the entire issue using pseudonyms, but this story proves to be mostly exaggerated. What is evident from Carver's time as editor is that *Toyon* was mainly under the authority of the students who ran it.

By 1966, *Toyon* had grown—literally—into a wider format, similar in size to a blue test book. 1966 was also the first appearance of labeled sections by genre, including art. Throughout the 1960s the book had illustrated covers and a center section called "portfolio of drawings," a small collection of line drawings by various artists. 1966 marked the first year that other forms of art were included, like photography, sculpture and oil paintings. This issue also denotes the role of 'Art Advisor,' a previously unheard of advisor suggesting that *Toyon* was trying to move in a new direction. Issues followed in this vein in the late 60s, ranging from experimental prose poems, simple line drawings and abstract cartoons, and interesting layout decisions. The play with pushing boundaries led to the controversial 1969 issue, featuring a nude woman on the cover, ending the decade on an explosive note and affirming that students had a firm hold of the direction *Toyon* would take for the next 40 years.

Volume 7, 1961

Volume 8, 1962

Class Standout

Best Mentor: Richard Cortez Day

Richard Cortez Day, or R.C. Day as was his regular publishing credit, was an author and professor at Humboldt State. Day was also a beloved member of the Arcata community and had a colored history throughout his life. Born in Kentucky and growing up in Michigan, he attended community college there before moving on to the University of Michigan, Ann Arbor to receive his B.S. in Math, and later his Masters in English Literature. He then served in the Navy before going back to school at the University of Iowa to receive his Ph.D. with a creative dissertation. Eventually, his love for the Pacific Ocean brought him to Arcata in 1959 where he began teaching English at Humboldt State.

Day taught for over 28 years at Humboldt and inspired a number of authors and writers within our community, including other People of *Toyon*, such as Raymond Carver and Jim Dodge. Day seemed to have been an initial influence on Carver's writing career as both played a part in *Toyon*'s history. Day was the *Toyon* advisor for several years during the same years Carver was editor, including volume 10, the infamous '63 Carver Coup (due to many of the short stories and poems being written by Raymond Carver himself and using the pseudonym John Vale).

Day was also an established author in his own right, published in several national literary journals, and two works of short stories and poetry. Day was truly appreciated for his accomplishment, and his love for the community was reciprocated after his first book *When In Florence*, sold 200 copies during an initial fan-signing at Northtown Books, a local bookstore in Arcata. His second book, *Something for the Journey*, touches on his love for the Arcata community as the synopsis describes a place not unlike the college town HSU resides in, "It was as though the residents of Winesburg, Ohio, had picked up, separately, and moved to the northern California coast."

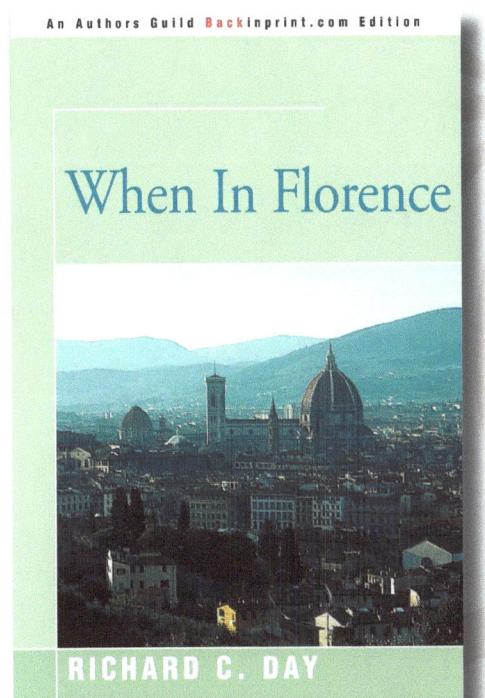

Day remained a supporter of *Toyon*, as a professor emeritus of Humboldt State University. According to his son, Cort Day, "Over the course of his career at Humboldt he combined the vocations of teaching and writing. In the 1960s and 1970s, he was instrumental in bringing major poets and writers to teach and read at Humboldt. Throughout his tenure, he supported *Toyon*, and he served as teacher, mentor, and guide to students with an interest in the art of fiction writing." In 2012, the Advisor's Award given to the best fiction piece, was renamed for Richard Cortez Day and generously funded by fellow professor emeritus, Jim Dodge.

The *Toyon* staff has RC Day to thank for the connection between the publication and organization to the English department. We often take for granted how closely connected the literary magazine is to our English department. Prior to the 1960s, the *Toyon* was essentially a student organization that ran itself, but with the edition of Professor Day to the faculty and with some of the talent of Raymond Carver, the *Toyon* began taking shape as an integral part of the literary scholarship of Humboldt students, as well as main characters in the history of *Toyon*.

-Additional writing by Joel Segura

Class Standout

Most Likely to Succeed: Raymond Carver

Unknown source, CC BY-SA 3.0, https://commons.wikimedia.org/w/index.php?curid=1824244

Of all of *Toyon*'s past contributors, Raymond Carver, the popular short story writer, is perhaps the best known. According to Carol Skelenicka's biography, *Raymond Carver: A Writer's Life*, Carver came to Humboldt State College in 1960, where he quickly formed a bond with professor Richard Cortez Day, who served as the faulty advisor to *Toyon*. *Toyon* proved to be a key factor in Carver's time at Humboldt State, when in Spring of 1961, his short story "My Father," was featured which, along with a simultaneous publication in Chico, was the first time Carver had been published. Carver continued pursuing writing and went on to serve as *Toyon*'s editor in 1963, publishing three more of his own short stories and one poem before leaving Arcata.

Volume 9, 1963

The 1963 edition of *Toyon,* which Carver edited, contains two pieces credited to him. However, Carver actually published four pieces in the magazine, two of which are under the pseudonym John Vale. Carver didn't even bother to hide the fact that John Vale was a pseudonym, writing "John Vale is a pseudonym of an H.S.C. [Humboldt State College] who wishes to remain anonymous" in the contributor's biography. This issue of *Toyon* only has seven contributors, contains a noticeably larger font that other issues, and is perhaps the only issue featuring a piece, a Brecht quote, explicitly labeled in the table of contents as "filler."

The journal had to live up to Carver's high expectations, and as a result he filled it with his own work and limited the number of other people published. Richard Cortez Day later recalled in his tribute to Carver, "Bad News," published in the 1989 issue, "He says there's not enough good stuff to fill the issue, so…he'll fill it with his own work, using various names. I say, 'It's skulduggery, but probably not felonious.'" Carver did as he said, filling roughly 46% of the 1963 issue with his own material.

Volume 10, 1964

Volume 11, 1965

Although the *Toyon* proved instrumental for Carver, and he in turn generated interest for the magazine, the ethos of the *Toyon* has changed over time, almost as a response to Carver. Though a writer, Carver did not graduate Humboldt with an English degree. As evidenced by Humboldt's 1963 graduation pamphlet, Carver opted for General Studies to avoid the year of foreign language required by the English department, which conflicts with *Toyon*'s current orientation as a multilingual journal.

It is important to acknowledge Carver as a key part of *Toyon*'s history, but it is also important to note that *Toyon* has changed. The 1964 issue, published the year after he left, features twice the number of contributors and has more space for writing with a smaller font. Carver's huge legacy overshadows the other contributors who worked with him on the 1963 issue, including Barbra Flora, who later went on to edit in 1964. Though these contributors never became as famous, their work is just as valuable, and just as much a part of Toyon's past as Carver's.

-**Dean Engle,**

Originally published on Toyonliterarymagazine.org

Volume 12, 1966

Volume 13, 1967

Volume 14, 1968

Pushing the Boundaries: The 1969 Issue

The 1969 edition of *Toyon* was particularly notable as a break in the more conservative attitude of the journal and HSC in general because of its notorious cover design. Unique from other less-ambitious covers, the cover photograph by Dale McKinnon, portrays a completely naked woman standing next to a fully clothed man under the canopy of the redwoods. Editors Steven Phipps, Joseph Fusco, and photo editor, Thomas Cooper kept their intentions for the cover from then faculty advisor, Ralph Samuelson. A 1991 article, written by Barbara Kelly, shone some light on the situation: Samuelson says he "did not know about the cover, and trusted Steven." After the issue was released it quickly became the most popular issue of *Toyon* and the only one to sell out.

Viewed through a modern lens it has been perceived as a sexist display of male supremacy, garnered through the fact that the woman is naked while the male fully clothed. Strides in feminist and gender theory have led to more discussion on the sexualization of women for entertainment and the exploitation of women through media, but it's important to note that in 1969 the cover was more of a nod towards the counter culture movement of the late 1960s, rather than a nefarious exploitation of the female body. According to Steven Phipps, who spoke to our editorial team in 2018, the choice of this cover was made to move away from the conservatism of the school and to reflect the new radical ideas being embraced by the student body.

The editors were very much aware of what they were doing and anticipated the kind of push back that would occur since Arcata was a conservative town (at the time). They took the editorial freedom they were given, had a friend take the photo and published it as the cover. Phipps also said that the editorial team had to go through a different publishing shop in order to get the cover published. It was kept a secret from most people until the release.

After copies had already been printed and on the way to present the book to sponsors, Samuelson was surprised to see the end result. "I had a last desperate thought of ripping off every cover, but that, too, seemed ridiculous, and I left it in the hands of destiny."

Volume 15, 1969

Phipps says the 1969 issue was supposed to be somewhat satirical about the student population of the time. The school, and *Toyon*, had been stodgy in the past. When asked if he knew that this issue is currently viewed as sexist because the woman is naked and the man is clothed, Phipps said, "It was in no way meant to be sexist nor viewed as sexist at the time. In fact, women adopted this counterculture of the "Humboldt Hunnie." Editors were trying to be radical enough to shake the norm by publishing a cover that featured the first naked person in *Toyon*. The 60s were replete with counterculture, protests, more liberal ways of thinking. It's not uncommon that students would be criticizing conservative ideas at the time. Phipps continues, "the woman wanted very much to be in the photo. She wanted to make a statement herself. It was liberating."

It's difficult to contend with history that doesn't always line-up with the social mores and political climate of the moment. While the most recent decade has been defined by the "me too" movement and call-out culture, where victims are empowered to become survivors and are using art, literature, film, and music to fight against a misogynistic society, the 1960s was very much about disrupting social norms, albeit in a different way. The staff of the 1969 issue were trying to push boundaries and shake up their small conservative school on the lost coast. The idea was to shock and break out of the power structures that were. The woman in the picture was championing herself as a "Humboldt hunnie," a title women used to denote reclaiming their power by owning their sexuality and bodies. The cover was meant to be an example of liberation, not an exploitation of women's bodies. We might question why only she was naked but we miss the point in thinking that nudity is inherently sexual although there is nothing sexual about the cover. The editors meant to make a statement and depict young people representing that counter-culture.

To conclude, "It certainly offended people, but that was not the point. It was not meant to offend women. We were making fun of the way of the conservative thinkers," says Phipps. The editors were trying to shock people in the community as a way of pushing back against the conservative climate. "We considered ourselves forward-thinking, and for Humboldt it was a liberating experience. It was a rather dull college before that."

-With contributions from Heather Rumsey, Quinn Dobbins, and Korinza Shlanta

The 1970s

1970
- This issue included an illustrated poster of nude women.

1971
- Format makeover: issues in 1971 and 1972 are wider but shorter and contain art that fills almost every page and 2-page spread.
- A poem by Stephen Fountain features a color label from the Oberti Olive Co. These labels were available in every issue, according to the editor's note.

1972
- Humboldt State College becomes California State University, Humboldt.

1973
- Editor's Cracks: advises future editors to know exactly how much financial backing you have for Toyon before you begin. -Kristen Atkinson

1974
- California State University, Humboldt is renamed Humboldt State University (finally one that sticks).
- Editor's Enlightenment: "Twice is enough"- Kristen Atkinson

1975
- Jim Dodge makes his first appearance as faculty advisor.

1977
- Art is printed in section of glossy paper in the middle of the book.

1978
- This volume contains a litany of misspelled thank you's to everyone from Captain Beefheart (twice), Allan Ginsberg [sic], John Lennin [sic], to Albert Einstein, Thomas Edison, and the-whole-left-wing. Unclear if misspellings are intentional. The back cover contains the exclamation "ON GAURD!" [sic].

1979
- The GWPE (Graduate Writing Proficiency Exam) is introduced to the Cal State system, effectively annoying English majors for decades.
- Jayne Anne Phillips serves as the Toyon advisor, one of the most celebrated writers with connections to Toyon. Phillips has won the Pushcart prize, Sue Kaufman Prize for First Fiction, and the Heartland Prize. She is the founder of the creative writing MFA at Rutgers University in New Jersey, where she also teaches.

The Seventies: Here Comes the Art

Much like the 1960s, which was full of air of civil unrest and a gradual acceptance of more "radical" values, the 1970s in America continued to find its voice, and Humboldt was no exception. Humboldt State College went through a brief identity crisis, becoming California State University-Humboldt in 1972 and settling on Humboldt State University in 1974. By 1975, the Vietnam War had ended, President Nixon had resigned, and an economic downturn was threatening the livelihoods of millions of Americans.

Volume 16, 1970

Volume 17, 1971

Volume 18, 1972

1970s

At Humboldt State, Toyon was struggling to find its place. Now nearly 20 years old, the 1970s was a time of experimentation for Toyon, both in tone and submissions. Editor's notes from the era are full of high ideals and frustrations with cash flow that keeps most small publications small. Editors tried on the name The Toyon Review for a few years starting in 1969, losing this title for a few years, then bringing it back in 1974 only for the moniker to disappear from view. Dynamic faculty advisors and creative writing professors of the 1970s including Jim Dodge, Judith Minty, Jorie Graham, Jim Galvin, and Jayne Anne Phillips helped to guide editors in their experimentation.

A major change to the future of Toyon came in the form of Art, with a capital "A." While the magazine always featured some simple sketches or line illustrations, it wasn't until the 1970s that the book started to include other mediums. Photography began to feature in Toyon in the late 60s and painting, sculpture, and mixed media emerged in the 70s. The magazine was taking art more seriously in conjunction to the prose already being published. In the 1971 issue, the editors

Volume 19, 1973

Volume 20, 1974

Volume 21, 1975

implored future editors to take more art into consideration and push the limits of format, layout, and graphic design to include art that reflects the written work.

"We want to leave some advice for the editors that will follow us. One of the first things we did as Editor was to go to the Library Archives and look up the previous issues of TOYON. Perusing them was a bore. Page after page was filled with print alone, and generally the graphic work was segregated from the literary work. Where graphics appeared in conjunction with the written work, they were usually unrelated. A superficial understanding of the photo offset printing process yields the information that any line art work (any work done in black and white only, with no gray) can be pasted on the page to be photographed at the same time as the written copy at no extra cost. We decided that this unused potential could be best exploited by assigning literary work to artists for illustration, with the artist drawing the artwork to the requirements of a specific poem or prose work. We also determined to illuminate every page of the magazine this way. Along with this revolutionary (for TOYON) procedure, we

Volume 22, 1976

determined that the magazine should have, as much as possible, a unified visual and intellectual design for each two facing pages. Our success in carrying out these policies is for others to judge. We are content to have broken new ground and set new standards for those who will follow us."
The Editor, "The Editorial WE," Toyon 71

This is an important change to Toyon's trajectory, considering the journal later defines itself as "a journal for the creative arts" and strives to include as much art as possible. The 1970s era of Toyon is a distinct emergence of a dynamic, student-run publication that actively sought to make use of their power and offer a space for artists and writers to make a statement.

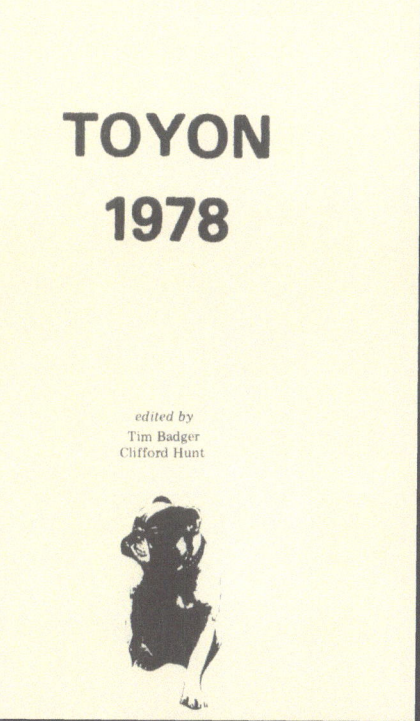

Volume 23, 1977 **Volume 24, 1978** **Volume 25, 1979**

Class Standout

Most Likely to Become a Professor: Jim Dodge

Jim Dodge and Laurie Pinkert at a Toyon release party in the 2000s

Jim Dodge has possibly the longest history with Toyon as anyone mentioned in these pages. His first encounter came in 1965 when his poem was featured in Toyon during his undergraduate career. Dodge came to Humboldt State College originally as a Fisheries Management major, but quickly changed course to writing and poetry, and graduated with an interdisciplinary degree in English, journalism, and biology. He then left Humboldt for the renowned Iowa Writer's Workshop, where he earned his MFA in Poetry in 1969.

Degrees in hand, Dodge returned to the west coast and Humboldt State University in the 1970s. In 1975, Dodge served as faculty advisor for Toyon and remained so for a few more years. As a result Toyon had a somewhat more stable appearance, no more major changes in style or format. Jim Dodge and other advisors seemed to guide student editors towards their ideas and creativity, allowing them the freedom to explore the possibilities of the magazine, despite financial issues. Jim Dodge spent some of his adult life on a commune in Sonoma County and his experiences with a variety of odd jobs from apple picker to teacher to environmental restorer influences his writing work, which mixes fantasy and folklore. He has published three full length novels (available in the Author's Hall at the HSU Library) and a selection of poems and prose in Rain on the River. His poetry and essays have been published in Toyon several times.

Dodge continued to teach English and creative writing at Humboldt State, maintaining a relationship with the English-department-sponsored Toyon. You could owe the continued life of Toyon to the relationships Dodge built, but there are hundreds more student editors and staff, and contributors from all over the world who have supported Toyon through the years. While Dodge is an inimitable figure in Toyon history, as well as the history of HSU and Humboldt, the magazine is first and foremost led by the students who put it together.

Dodge seemed to understand this and focused on allowing the staff to lead the charge with Toyon: designing the covers, table of contents, and hand selecting each piece that appears. In 1995, Dodge became the head of the Creative Writing program at HSU and once again took over the reins of advisor. Dodge recognized how this student publication allowed HSU students to get a firsthand experience with publishing and editing, and so was instrumental in creating ENGL 460 as a course in literary publishing. Dodge continued to support Toyon into the new millennium and even after his retirement in 2014. As professor emeritus he generously has funded the Richard Cortez Day Award for Fiction and continues to support Toyon whenever he can. Jim Dodge still lives in Northern California.

The 1980s

1980

- This year's issue has a pale salmon paper cover with "TOYON '80" on it. There is no art on the cover and very little in the issue.

1982

- This year's issue has a paper cover with "Toyon 82" on it and art at bottom. This issue includes a picture of a toyon bush courtesy of HSU Botany professor, James P. Smith Jr. The picture is accompanied by the following explanation:
- "Toyon was first published in 1954 and annually since 1957. Charles Bloom, who is currently HSU's head of Information Services, suggested that name *Toyon* to Bev Dahlen, editor of the magazine in 1954. Even though the Toyon bush—photinia hetereomeles arbutifolia isn't native to the immediate HSU vicinity, Ms. Dahlen found the word to be an appropriate title because of its euphony."

1983

- Beloved *Toyon* and HSU alum, Jodi Stutz, serves as assistant editor and editor in 1984. Poet and professor at College of the Redwoods in Eureka, CA, David Holper is editor-in-chief.
- *Toyon* utilizes Bug Press in Arcata for printing. Holper and Stutz laid out pages by hand for printing.

1984

- Toyon turns 30! Jodi Stutz celebrates the achievement in the editor's note.
- The Raymond Carver Short Story contest is established and runs for the first time.

- The award, originally funded by Carver himself, attracted hundreds of submissions from around the world, accepting over nine hundred entries in 1993. According to Holper, Jodi Stutz got Carver's contact information from a professor and cold-called him about creating a contest in his honor, convinced by a bold Stutz, he sent her a check for the first prize. Submissions were reviewed by HSU students and judged by a different established author every year. The winners were published in the *Toyon* and awarded a five hundred dollar cash prize. The contest would go on to become a class (ENGL 470, first offered in 1993) that students could take for credit, screening the submissions. The award remained active until 2005.
- Acknowledgments page includes a staff photo for the first time in *Toyon* history.

1985

- Along with contributors and acknowledgments, the magazine also features adverts for local businesses—most likely in an effort to fundraise for publication costs.

1987

- The issue this year includes staff names and positions and publication info; this issue also lists the Raymond Carver Short Story Contest board for the first time. The contest was typically advertised with posters and mailed brochures, although it is unclear who they were sent to.

1988

- Volume 34 "In memory of Jodi Stutz, 1958-1987" reprinting of her short story "Prairie Hearts" with acknowledgment of her contribution to Toyon.

- Raymond Carver dies in August of this year.

1989

- Volume 35 is dedicated to "Raymond Carver Toyon Editor 1963' and "In Memory of Michelle Kagan Toyon Editor 1964."

- This issue includes a reprinting of a 1963 Raymond Carver story, along with a memorial for Carver by R.C. Day.

Volume 27, 1981

Volume 26, 1980

The Eighties: The Me Decade vs. the Editorial We

Looking at the 1980s editions of Toyon, there is a sense of cohesion that borders on professionalism. This isn't to say that it wasn't a dynamic magazine still full of the spark of youth, just that the 1980s took an undoubtedly conservative turn socially and politically that can be felt in the aesthetics of *Toyon*. The 1980s are sometimes collectively known as the "me decade" or even as the age of greed. It is after all, the era of Ronald Reagan, the greed of "Wall Street" main antihero Gordon Gecko, and cool conservatives like Alex P. Keaton from the sitcom "Family Ties." Despite attempts to appeal to Americans ready to go back to the prosperity of the post-war 50s, there were equally advancements in feminism, gay rights, and continuing anti-establishment rebellion mostly due in part to the conservatism promoted in Reaganomics and the UK's own Iron Lady, Margaret Thatcher. There was a healthy faction of defectors to the mainstream culture and there sat *Toyon*, on a precipice of social activism.

According to former 80s-era editor, David Holper, the operation of *Toyon* was still very much a fly-by-the-seat-of-your-pants collection, put together by a group of students hand-selected by faculty and their friends who were interested in helping out. But under the surface is a growing cohesion. For example, editors were asked up to a year ahead to take up the editor-in-chief role, serving as an assistant editor in the edition prior—a practice still in use today. The books started to become slightly more connected by having similar front matter pages listing the staff, their roles, and table of contents. Although there was some variation in this over the decade, it at least points towards the next part of *Toyon*'s history in the 1990s.

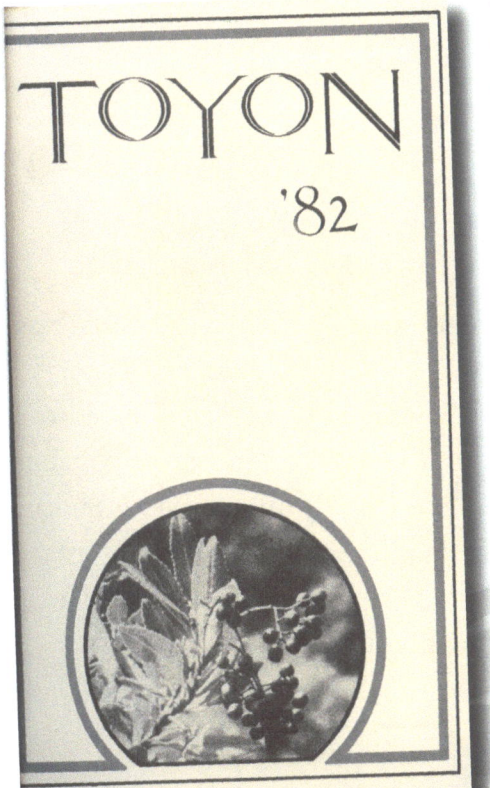

Volume 28, 1982

The 1984 Toyon staff

In the mid-80s when *Toyon* hit one of its major milestones, with 30 years of history, Jodi Stutz was on board as editor. The issue Stutz edited focuses on *Toyon's* history, where the matter of history is rarely touched on before the 1980s; this suggests *Toyon* was beginning to be taken a little more seriously than before. While the magazine was years from becoming a for-credit class, the passions of the students drove the book along. It was Stutz's spunk that led to the Raymond Carver Short Story contest that quickly grew to one of the most popular offerings in *Toyon* for years to come. It could be argued that the strength and draw of Carver is what kept this relatively small student publication alive throughout the 80s and into the 1990s, ensuring the future that was to come.

In 1984, the Raymond Carver Short Story Contest began its two-decade run. But the short story contest wasn't created by anyone trying to boost their status, or even to win much-needed funds for production. Instead it was started the way any other award or contest *Toyon* has hosted in the past: because a student had an idea and had the enterprising nature to see it through. Jodi Stutz was that kind of dynamic student that thrived on *Toyon*. Stutz's friend and colleague David Holper today still speaks highly of his experience with *Toyon*, crediting the publication with turning him from student to professional writer. Being exposed to professional writers the creative writing faculty were able to bring to campus, combined with the hands-off approach of faculty advisors towards the editors of *Toyon*, allowed Holper and others the freedom to hone their skills and find their way into the writing and publishing world.

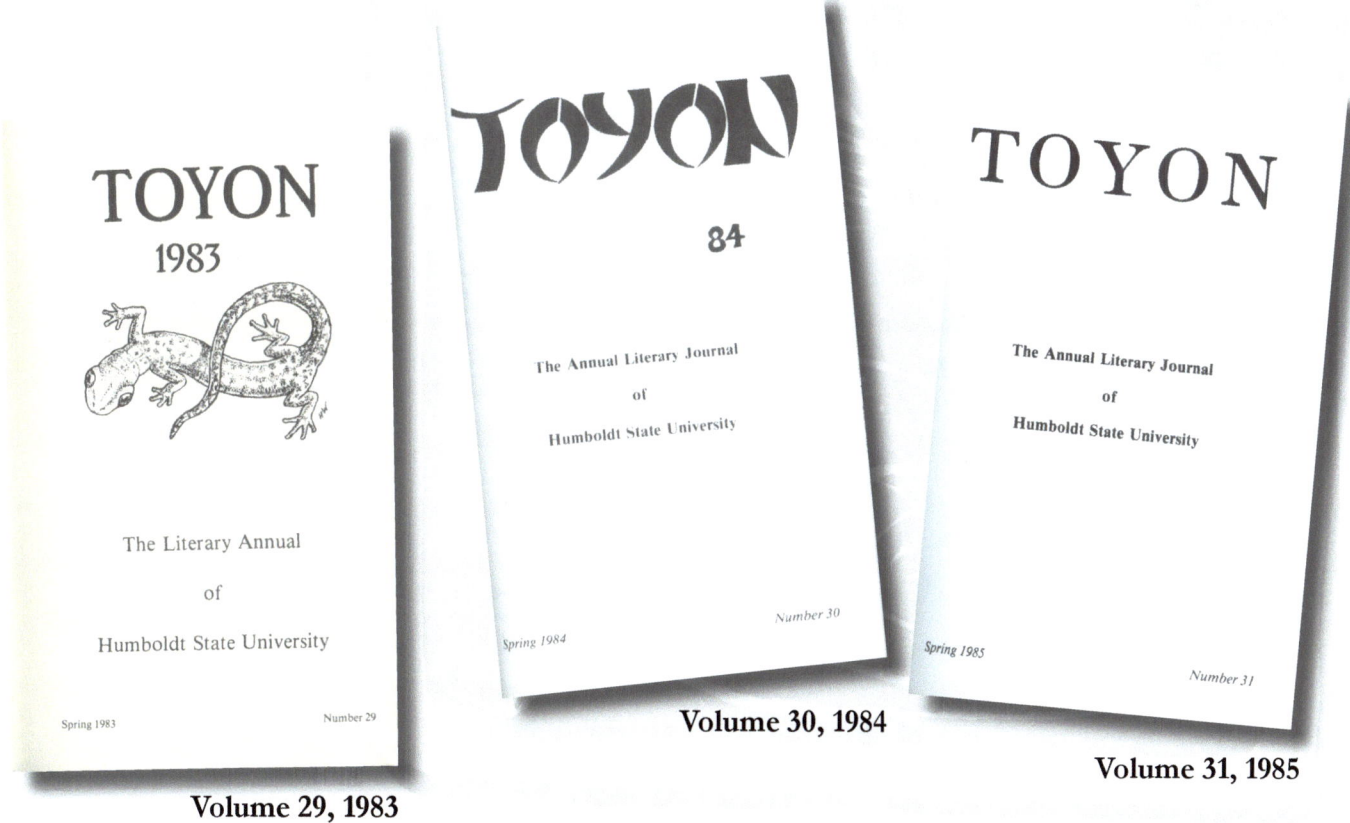

Volume 29, 1983

Volume 30, 1984

Volume 31, 1985

The 1980s saw a shift from *Toyon* being a student activity to it being a training ground for future writers, artists, editors, and publishers. Raymond Carver, a *Toyon* alum, was quickly becoming a darling in short story writing, being compared to Hemingway. It was the first bona fide celebrity to have been birthed by *Toyon* and that seemed to have affected what *Toyon* was to become over the next 30 years.

Class Standout

The Poet Laureate: David Holper

Photo with permission from Eric Furman

Despite the *Toyon* poetry award being named for Jodi Stutz, it is her co-editor from 1983, David Holper, that has been named the City of Eureka's first Poet Laureate in 2019. Holper came to Humboldt State at the end of the 1970s, a Journalism-turned-English major when he was asked by Jorie Graham and Jim Galvin, married writing professors, to help edit *Toyon*. Holper remembers enlisting his writer friends to fill in the rest of the editorial board. The advisors were mainly hands-off which meant Holper was free to hire friends to illustrate the cover and editorial meetings and selections were held in someone's living room over beers.

It's *Toyon* and the creative writing faculty that Holper credits with turning him into a writer. He says prior to the exposure to the writers that came to visit Humboldt State he didn't feel like a "real writer." Working for *Toyon* put Holper in a behind-the-scenes role that allowed him to see writing from another angle. Encouraged by the faculty of the English department and his experience as the managing editor led him to pursue an MFA at the University of Massachusetts, Amherst. Holper has continued to teach English and creative writing at College of the Redwoods in Eureka. He also works as the faculty advisor for the literary journal at the school, *Seven Gill Shark Review*. Much like *Toyon*, *Seven Gill Shark Review* is helmed by the students who make selections for the magazine and organize the release party. In this way David helps *Toyon*'s influence spread to future generations.

Holper has published two books of poetry, *The Bridge* (Sequoia Song Publishing) and *64 Questions* (March Street Press). He continues to support *Toyon* and has been published in its pages over the years. He has been a great source of first-hand experiences and stories from *Toyon* in the 1980s to anecdotes about his "full of piss-and-vinegar" colleague, Jodi Stutz.

Class Standout

Patron Saint of Toyon: Jodi Stutz

Jodi Lee Stutz was born in Minnesota and grew up in the Midwest. Jodi is the namesake for the annual poetry award after her life was tragically cut short in 1987, just three years after she graduated HSU with a B.A. in English.

She ended up in Humboldt via Los Angeles and an incident at the John Deere main office. The story goes that in 1980, at the ripe age of 21, Jodi was working for John Deere as a secretary where they had one of the first commercial Xerox copy machines in the area. The technology of photocopies was a relatively new and exciting component to an otherwise quiet office. Jodi enlisted another secretary to act as a lookout as she pulled her pants down and took perfect copies of her bare behind. When her bosses discovered her indiscretion she was fired.

This could otherwise be an anecdote of office hi-jinks in the 1980s, except the story was picked up by nationally syndicated columnist Bob Greene who effectively caused Stutz a brief 15-minutes of fame. Not only was she a part of Johnny Carson's monologue during three nights that week, she was also invited to LA to be a part of a news magazine to talk about the event. A few short years later Jodi

The ID cards of Jodi Stutz

The 1985 Toyon Staff

made her way to HSU and made her stamp on *Toyon* in 1983 as assistant editor and managing editor in 1984.

Professor David Holper, *Toyon* managing editor in 1983, remembers her fondly, "Jodi was bright, energetic, feisty, fun, and a people magnet. She was not afraid in the least to speak her mind, and given what happened at John Deere with the copy machine, you can tell she didn't care too much for social conventions. She was determined to become a successful writer, and I am confident that had she lived, we would now be reading her work and admiring it."

Jodi was a prolific writer, writing three book length manuscripts and several poems, while attending HSU and later CSU Long Beach for her graduate degree. She published numerous explicit and erotic stories in Forum, Fling, and Penthouse under a pen name and personal correspondence in Humboldt State's archives' possession suggests she even taught classes on how to write erotic stories.

Jodi Stutz very much embodies the *Toyon* spirit. She was a bright, funny, and bold young woman. By reading her editor's note in the 1984 volume, her unique voice and personality shines through. Stutz was unafraid to reach out to Raymond Carver to ask for money to start the Raymond Carver Short Story contest, one of the most enduring awards in *Toyon*'s history. She also was cognizant of the role of *Toyon* as an institution. Her letter makes note of the 30 year history of the magazine and her attempts at doing good by the ol' girl for her 30th birthday.

Just prior to her tragic death, Stutz was working tirelessly to find an agent and publisher for her collection of short stories, *Blue Ribbon* and her novel, *The Andalusian Cowgirl*. She also wrote an account of her fifteen minutes of fame titled *It was Only a Paper Moon*. She had just moved to the small Minnesota town of Currie for a quiet place to write but was unfortunately hit by a bullet while reading in her apartment. A fight in her front yard, unrelated to her, resulted in her accidental death.

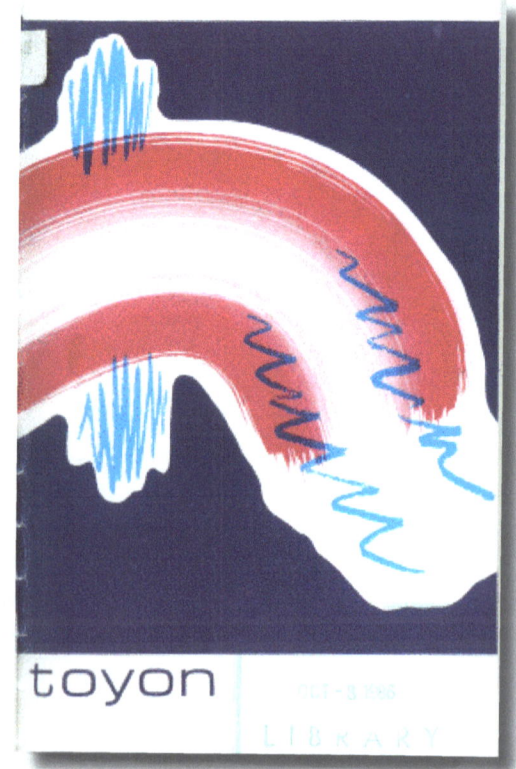

Volume 32, 1986

Volume 33, 1987

Volume 34, 1988 **Volume 35, 1989**

Toyon dedicated the 1987 edition to Jodi and reprinted her story "Prairie Hearts." Her collected works can be viewed by appointment in Special Collections at the Humboldt State University Library.

Further reading: Greene, Bob. "She was an Original, Not a Photocopy." https://www.chicagotribune.com/news/ct-xpm-1987-06-24-8702160831-story.html

Van Hooker, Brian. "A Very Important Cultural History of People Photocopying Their Butts" https://melmagazine.com/en-us/story/a-very-important-cultural-history-of-people-photocopying-their-butts

"Man Charged In Death Of Woman Fired For Photocopy Prank" https://www.apnews.com/7aff24833ff713dfd96d5f8a2f1900bb

TOYONLORE

The Changing Names of Toyon

Is it a Journal or a Magazine?

The question had bubbled over the first few weeks of the semester. As new people joined the *Toyon* staff in the Fall of 2018, there was some time spent being quizzed on the history of our robust little magazine. As members of the group of students tasked with designing and editing the 65th edition of the book, we were expected to table for our publication, going to the quad with a stack of old issues and stickers armed with the knowledge we crammed over the last few class periods to talk to other students, professors, staff and anyone else who might stop by about *Toyon* and how to submit. The same issue came up time and again, "what do you call it? A magazine? A literary journal?" and everyone had different answers. Some staff members just called it a "creative arts journal," for clarity and conciseness. Others used "literary journal" to mark the seriousness with which we approach our publication. There simply didn't seem to be a consensus about what we were called and for a few months, it didn't matter too much. There were already hundreds of stickers emblazoned with "Toyon Literary Magazine" and staff member business cards we passed out with our contact info proclaimed "Toyon: Multilingual Journal of Literature and Art." There didn't seem to be cohesion there, so maybe it didn't matter what we called it, only that we were talking about it and often.

As the semester wore down and we began reaching the final decisions about what was going to be included and what would be axed, the topic was broached again. This time we were looking at mock-ups for potential cover art and our design leads had included the title "Toyon Lit Mag." I won't say the battle was waged, but the staff got into a very spirited discussion that I'm embarrassed to admit went on for nearly 30 minutes over whether we were a journal or a magazine. There were fears that "literary journal" or anything using "journal," was too stuffy and too reminiscent of English departments of old that centered the white male writer. There was the equally valid thought that "lit mag," was far too juvenile if we wanted to be taken seriously, but this only led to another argument about how serious we should take ourselves. Almost every member of our staff spoke up and offered another revision or caveat to the terms.

In the end, the discussion was tabled indefinitely. The 65th edition was published as Toyon Lit Mag, as was fitting with the retro look of the cover. On the inner title page it is printed as "Humboldt State University's Multilingual Literary Magazine," so I assume we will just have to wait for the book to evolve again as new students take on the reins.

The 1990s

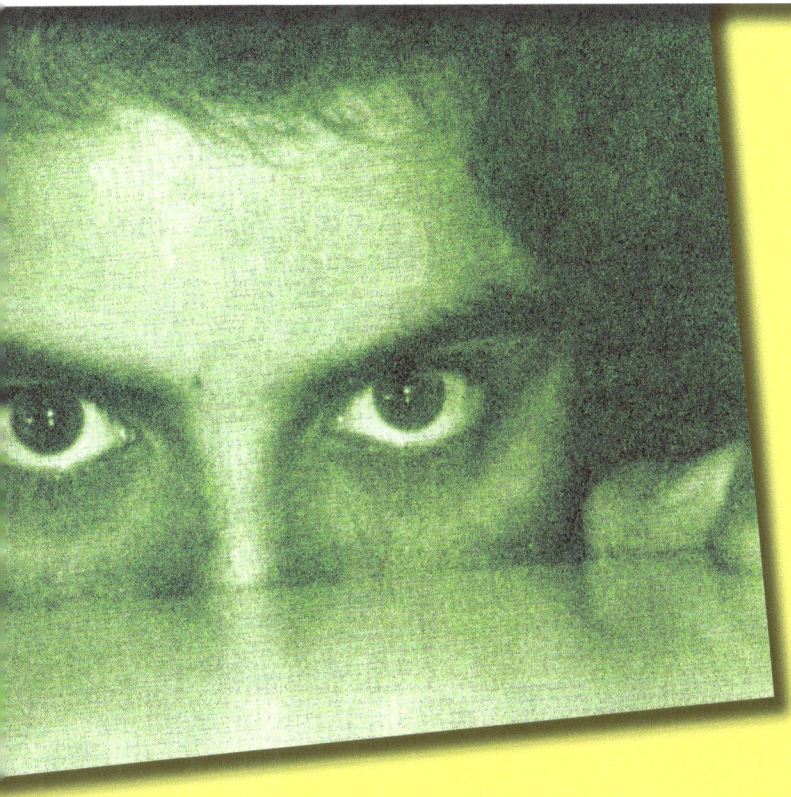

1990
- There is no visual art in this volume.
- There are 20 different published pieces but only 14 contributors.

1991
- Volume 37 is one of the most circulated editions of *Toyon* because of its coastal, blue cover.
- This issue contains a Contributor's Note in the back of volume along with the authors' bios.

1993
- Volume 39 was a poetry-heavy edition.
- This volume is dedicated to Judith Minty, "who helped so many young poets find their voice."

1994
- In contrast to the previous edition, volume 40 was prose-heavy.

1995
- There were two volumes of *Toyon* published in Fall and Spring of this year. Volume 41 was dedicated to the horror genre.
- There is a definition of what a toyon is: It is what we call the California Holly Tree.
- The back has a dedication to Judith Minty for being the Final Judge of the Raymond Carver Short Story Contest. There is a lovely broomstick under the dedication, a nice call back to the previous edition's theme.

1996
- This edition included an incredible variety of text fonts. Most entries include a stylized title, text and pulled quotes from said entry. The text style varied from piece to piece. This staff's typesetter must have been a magician.

1997
- *Toyon* did not publish this year. This is the first of only two total occurrences of a issue not being published annually.

1998

- *Toyon* is back and under the advisement of Dan Levinson, who had been the advisor since 1996.
- This volume marks the start of a trend that last well into the 2000's: the inclusion of title page epigraphs. The first being: "Art when really understood is the province of every human being. It is simply a question of doing things, anything, well." - Robert Henri
- The Jodi Stutz Memorial Award first appeared in this volume. The first winner was Dawn McCulloch for their poem "Small Victory."

1999

- This volume sees the first appearance of the Advisor's Award, which is later renamed the Richard Cortez Day award: (see 2012 timeline entry). The first winner of this recognition is Kendra Dwelley for "Washer Woman." The award is funded by former *Toyon* advisor Jim Dodge till this day.
- *Toyon i*s officially a part of the HSU curriculum with the creation of ENGL 460, originally created as a two-unit class.
- Volume 45 was dedicated to: "The advisors, editors, and associates dedicated this volume to SHERRON "Sherry" DABROWSKI, former HSU student, local artist, and good soul who died March 11, 1999. The body melts away but your spirit lives on in those who love you."

Volume 36, 1990

Class Standout

Patron of the Arts:

Dr. Barbara Brinson Curiel

Anyone that has spent any significant amount of time in the English or Critical Race and Gender Studies departments has heard wonderful whisperings of Dr. Barbara Brinson Curiel. Chicana poet and 2012 winner of the Philip Levine Prize for Poetry for her poetry book *Mexican Jenny and Other Poems,* Barbara has dedicated her career to the teaching and creation of Latinx literature. In 1997, Barbara started her professorship at Humboldt, in which soon after she became involved with *Toyon*. After Jim Dodge retired from HSU, she became the Faculty Advisor for the Raymond Carver Short Story Contest (RCSSC). The contest was unique since it was at the forefront of the literary contest wave that started emerging in the early 2000s. She recalls how popular the contest was, with its numerous submissions, and how it was the start to many emerging writers.

After the RCSSC ended, Barbara stayed connected to *Toyon* in a variety of different ways. As a professor of creative writing, she encouraged her students to start their journey in publishing within their local community and submit to not only *Toyon* but other publications housed on campus like *The Matrix a*nd *The Multicultural Times,* to name a few. She imparted to her students the ways in which *Toyon* can be a viable opportunity for those who want a taste of what it is like to be a published writer. Her consistent commitment to the creative process gained her the honor of having *Toyon*'s Multilingual Award renamed in her namesake in 2019. While Barbara admits that it was kind of the Toyon Staff to name an award after her, she tells of how her greatest contribution to *Toyon* was being part of the interview process that eventually led to the start of Dr. Janelle Adsit's position as Faculty Advisor for *Toyon* in 2015.

The act of writing is synonymous with community in Barbara's eyes. As a 2010-2012 CantoMundo Fellow and a Coordinating Committee member from 2013-2016, she engaged, and continues to do so, with other Latinx poets to create and build a solid community with poets who are often overlooked and underrepresented in the literary world. Since the 1970s, Barbara remembers other Latinx writers creating their own spaces outside of white-dominated writing spaces. Starting presses, publishing houses, and writer's workshops specifically for Latinx people continues to be a way in which writers no longer have to explain their experiences or existence. Or as Barbara puts it: "we can promote the values, vision, and the voice without having to explain, contextualize, translate or meet somebody else's criteria. And that's a really validating experience for writers."

Barbara's parting wisdom to her students and those who are eager to start their own journey in publishing is simple: find good teachers, build community and space for yourself whenever possible, and remember that writing is not just about the physical production—writing is testimony, so write like it.

The Nineties: From Minimalism to the New Millennium

Front & back of Volume 37, 1991, & 38, 1992

The 90s continued in the tradition of creating professional yet eclectic literary journals. Unlike the experimental 1980s, the beginning of this decade, staff members appeared to have taken a minimalist approach with not only its published material but the visual art between the pages. The first three editions saw no visual art within its pages, not even a line drawing. This lack of visual art within the pages did not deter staff members from creating two beautiful blue covers for volumes 37 (1991) and 38 (1992).

Dense with minimalist poetry, volume 39 (1993) featured almost exclusively poetry that consisted of 1 to 3 words per line, with little punctuation throughout, meant to look longer than the actual length of the poem on the page. This style has found new popularity with artists like Rupi Kaur and other contemporary poets. This convention twisting issue is also aptly dedicated to Judith Minty for helping "so many young poets find their voice."

The mid-to-late 90s would disrupt the modesty of the early 90's by publishing two separate editions in 1995. Under the advisement of Vince Gotera, volume 41 was dedicated to the genre of horror. Not only were the contents of this issue full of creepy and dark content, the staff of this issue integrated the genre to create a spooky twist to normal bookmaking conventions. With its table of contents retitled as "Innards," the Volume 41 staff called themselves "The Unforgiven" and those who were not editors "Readers, Assistants, and General Indentured Servants." Combined with its cover art and font choices, this volume pulled out all the scary tricks.

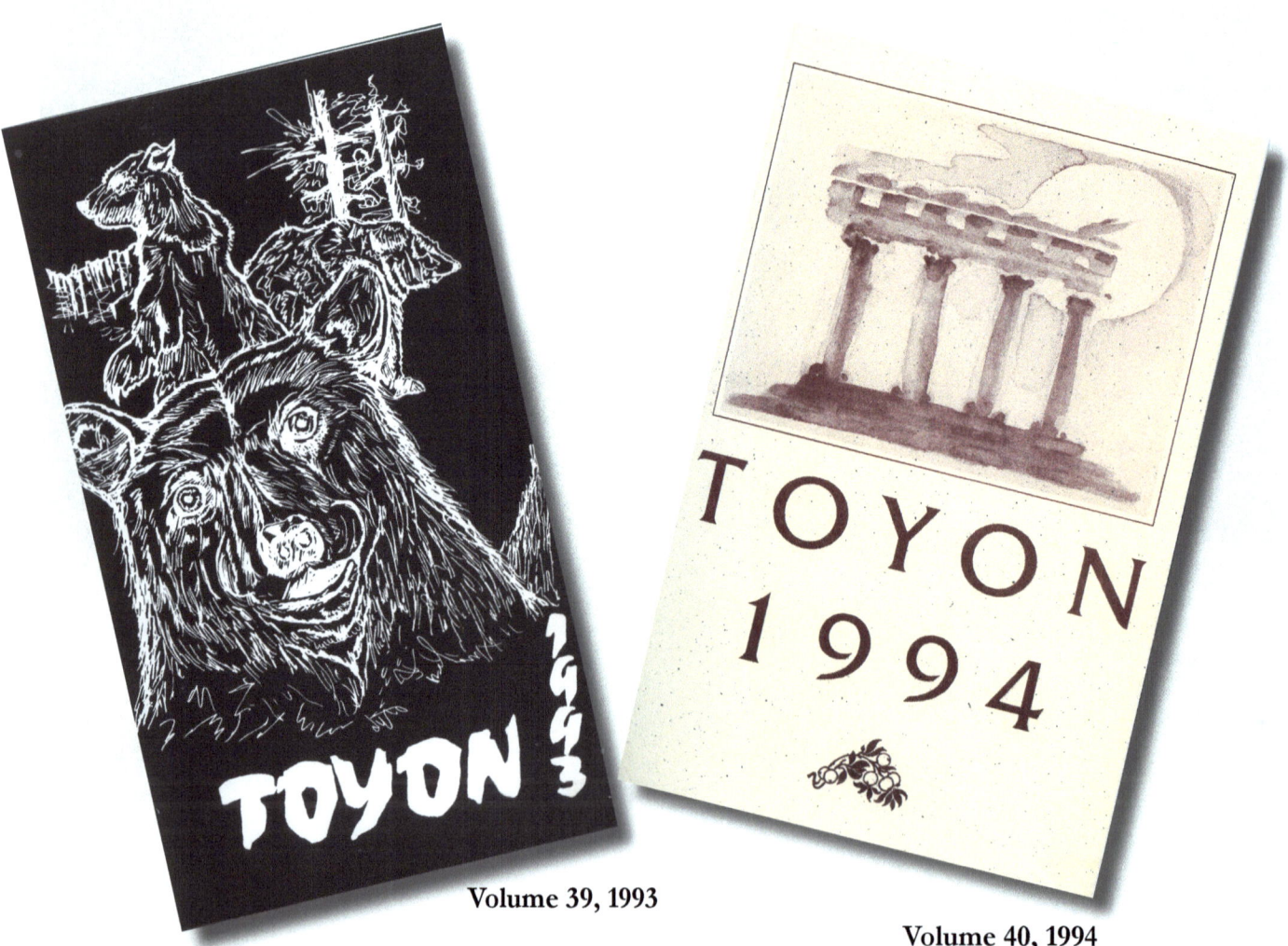

Volume 39, 1993

Volume 40, 1994

The next 1995 publication, volume 42, would find itself under a new faculty advisor, Kim Griswell. This volume is unique in size, reminiscent of the shape of a children's picture book. This issue was special because it had two winners for the Raymond Carver Short Story Contest. This volume also has a dedication to Judith Minty for her work as the final judge for the contest. A witch's broomstick drawing is placed under the dedication—a small acknowledgment to the previous issue's theme.

Volume 42, Spring 1995

Volume 41, Fall 1995

In 1996, volume 43 gracefully continued the creativity from the previous issues. With full length art pieces, pulled quotes from its content and several font styles, Volume 43 is possibly the only edition of *Toyon* to be printed entirely on glossy photo paper.

Interestingly the production of *Toyon* was halted in 1997, making it the second of two years in *Toyon*'s history not to publish an edition, the first being in 1955.

Volume 43, 1996

Volume 44, 1998

Toyon returned for volume 44 in 1998 with a new subtitle: Humboldt State University's Journal of Creativity. Dan Levinson, the faculty advisor at the time, managed to get the help the staff needed in order to finalize and publish the volume by asking for funding from different sources, one of them being from Jim Dodge, who took over as faculty advisor in 1999.

1990s

The last volume of the millennium saw the creation of ENGL 460, the class that to this day facilitates the production of *Toyon*. Created originally as a 2-unit class, ENGL 460 formalizes the production cycle of a book, allowing for more stability for its new staff members and allowing for consistency in the funding of the journal. The class would later become a four unit class after 2015, which allowed ENGL 460 to become not only a class but an internship-like experience for its staff members. Volume 45 was the first appearance of the Advisor's Award, renamed the Richard Cortez Day Award in 2012, which is still funded by Jim Dodge. The first winner of this award was Kendra Dwelley for their piece titled "Washer Woman." This volume was dedicated to Sherron "Sherry" Dabrowski which read: "former HSU student, local artist, and good soul who died March 11, 1999. The body melts away but your spirit lives in those who love you."

Volume 45, 1999

The 2000s

2000
- An Errata statement (denoting printing errors) included in the front matter.
- Title page epigraph read: "If you take any activity, any art, any discipline, any skill, take it and push it as far as it will go, push it beyond where it has ever been before, push it into the wildest edge of edges, then you force it into the realm of magic." -Tom Robbins
- Start of Sherri DeBrowski Award for Women in Diverse Media (2000-2009)

2001
- First appearance of guidelines for submissions for the following year printed in the book.
- This year's staff added to the guidelines the 1999 RSCSC Award winners underneath the 2000 winners.
- The Ruth Mountaingrove Award began (2001- 2010) for Best Poem in Traditional Form. The first piece to receive this recognition is "Sestina for Grace" by Melody King-Ulrich.

2003
- Volume 49 included an "Advisor's Apologia" in the front matter. Jim Doge wrote it as an apology for Toyon not printing a fiction piece in the edition.

2004
- This 50th anniversary edition was dedicated to Richard Cortez Day as a writer, teacher, mentor, and role model. This volume also includes a title epigraph: "Since time is the one immaterial object which we cannot influence—neither speed up nor slow down, add to nor diminish—it is an imponderably valuable gift." -Maya Angelou
- Linda L. Smith, coordinating editor, wrote a letter to the readers of Toyon. Fun Fact: 2004 saw the longest version of the Toyon publication up to this point in history, with 120 pages in the volume.

2005
- The Claire Elizabeth Chapman Memorial Award for best essay on overcoming adversity was established. Yet, there is no record that anyone ever received this award. It was listed as a possible award that could be won until 2007.

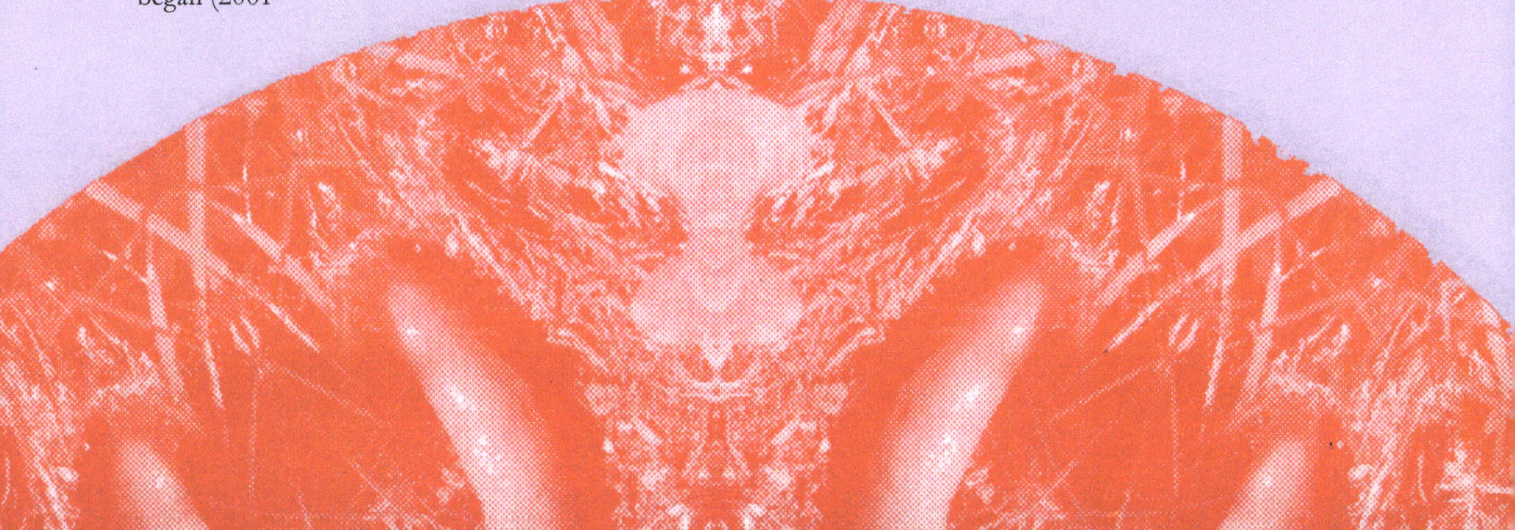

- The Redwood Empire Mensa Award was established (2005-2019). This award was for the best Creative Nonfiction piece.
- There are some nice stylistic choices in this volume's layout. Each entry's text is encased in a thin-black border and a decorative leaf design under each title.
- This was the last year that the Raymond Carver Short Story Contest was published.

2006

- The front matter includes a Advisory Notice written by Jim Dodge

2007

- This volume is dedicated to Jerry Martien: "budgeted into retirement, HSU loses a great writing teacher; fortunately the North Coast community retains an even greater writer."
- The staff is configured as a cooperative, a method that was meant to rid editorial hierarchies.

2008

- This volume marks the first time spoken word was included in an edition: "you should find a CD insert of North Coast spoken word artists performing their work."

2009

- On the Staff page there is a public shout-out to third-year cooperative editorial staff as being the: "Minions of Menial, the Bosses of the Boring, our Shepherds of Schlep, all the Fools of Facilitation…"
- A Note on the Advisor written by Jacob Lehman included a tongue and cheek note about Jim Dodge and his departure as Toyon's Faculty Advisor after 14 years.

Volume 46, 2000

The 2000s: Epigraphs and Ghost Awards

The world was able to make it to the 2000s without initiating the end of the world after the Y2k scare. Although computers failed to become our tech overlords, they still were the cause of the printing problems faced in volume 46. This issue included a piece of paper glued to each issue's cover called The Errata, short for erratum, which is a list of printing errors featured in the volume.

The first issue of the new decade also saw the start of a trend in most of the volumes published in the 2000s: epigraphs. These quotes were from various sources, some from popular writers; others include wisdom from past faculty advisors.

The 2000s saw numerous awards created, some are still around today. The first one being The Sherri DeBrowski Award for Women in Diverse Media, active from 2000 to 2009. Jim Dodge noted that:

"Sherri Debrowski was a student at HSU who was a member of the TOYON staff for two years. Shortly after graduating, she was diagnosed with breast cancer, and after a few years of struggling through treatment, she died unexpectedly of a cerebral hemorrhage. To honor her fine spirit and her courage, I initiated the award and thought I had an agreement with the Humboldt Community Breast Health Project (HCBHP) to fund it, but the HCBHP Board decided that it would violate their bylaws, particularly since the award was reserved for women (like Sherri) who display creativity in two artistic disciplines, and because Sherri had been something of a feminist, a political element was also present, and the HCBHP was worried that they were straying too far afield from their medical focus... I funded the prize personally for a few years, but eventually, for a variety of reasons, decided to just drop it."

Volume 47 included the first formal submission guidelines included in its pages along with the names of the 1995 (volume 45) winners of the Raymond Carver Short Story Contest Award. The winner's names did not make it into the volume they won in but two staff rotations after made sure they received their acknowledgments for winning.

Volume 47, 2001   **Volume 48, 2002**   **Back Cover Volume 48, 2002**

This volume was also the first to give the Ruth Mountaingrove Award, active from 2001 to 2010. This award, according to Jim Dodge, was made possible by:

> *"Ruth Mountaingrove [who] was an elder in the local poetry community who wanted to advance the interest in writing in traditional forms (sonnet, villanelle, sestina, and so on). She sent a $50 check each year that was awarded to the best poem in a traditional form."*

It is said that Ruth was on somewhat of a fixed income, but still wanted to support the continuation of traditional poetic form within the pages of Toyon.

In 2003, volume 49 included an Advisor's Apologia in the front matter of the issue. Written by Jim Dodge it states the reasons why the Toyon staff did not publish a fiction piece in the volume. The two reasons were:

> *(1) Fiction submissions were down from the year before, but poetry submissions were up.*
>
> *(2) All fiction submissions scored near a 7, not outstanding but good pieces. Staff decided they would rather "maintain the highest standards rather than make essentially arbitrary choices among the equally worthy."*

Volume 49, 2003

The 50th Anniversary of Toyon in 2004 featured a textured matte black cover with gold foil lettering on the cover. Dedicated to Richard Cortez Day "writer, teacher, mentor, and role model," this volume also received a subtitle change to Humboldt State University's Journal of Art and Literature. According to the Coordinating Editor of the volume, Linda L. Smith, the 50th Anniversary was the longest Toyon Publication to date, with 120 pages; the 65th volume in 2019 eventually dethroned this edition by at least 10 pages.

Volume 50, 2004

By 2005, another award was created but was never awarded. The Claire Elizabeth Chapman Memorial Award for best essay on overcoming adversity was established and remained listed as a possible award to be won until disappearing in 2007 without ever publishing a recipient. This is the same year that the Redwood Empire Mensa Award was established, although no one received this award until 2006. This award, sponsored by the local chapter of Mensa until 2019, was gifted to the best creative nonfiction submission in each annual volume.

In 2007, volume 53 was created with equity and some tongue and cheek activism in mind. According to 2018-2019 Creative Nonfiction Editor, Jasmine Nazario:

Volume 51, 2005

"The 2007 issue (volume 53) celebrates the student-led production of the Toyon we know and love today."

In the editorial statement, the masthead of twenty-one students enrolled in the class share with Toyon readers that their plan for volume 53 was to reduce any position that would generate hierarchical setbacks. The production of a literary magazine requires a great deal of collaboration and communication between departments. Because there are separate departments, the class wanted to ensure that miscommunication was something they could avoid overall by creating a "list of tasks and four main editorial boards, and people took responsibility for what appealed to them." Despite the breakdown of genres, each student had the opportunity to contribute their concerns and opinions during the production of volume 53. The faculty advisor for that year only took on the responsibility of ensuring deadlines were met, calling meetings and posting fliers.

Volume 52, 2006

Volume 53, 2007

Volume 54, 2008

For some, taking the Toyon class might be the first time ever being exposed to the publishing industry. The norm within the publishing industry is that the masthead is divided into departments that solely focus only on their specified tasks. The masthead for Toyon changes every year. It is from my knowledge as a current member of the 2018 masthead, that each year we aspire to do something special for each issue. The special something from the 2007 issue was the masthead's ability to produce a beautiful and complete issue of Toyon while challenging the conventions associated with publishing.

Volume 53 featured a dedication to Professor Jerry Martien who was "budgeted into retirement, HSU loses a great writing teacher; fortunately, the North Coast community retains an even greater writer."

The volume 54 (2003) of Toyon produced a volume that included a CD in each journal with Spoken Word artists from the North Coast performing their work. According to a past Toyon Staff member, Toyon has always been engaged with Spoken Word in the community as far back as the 70s. However, the genre was not formalized into Toyon until the second half of the 2010s.

A galley proof of Volume 52

By the end of the 2000s, Toyon was in its third year of its cooperative editors organizational structure, to celebrate this the staff included a public shout out to themselves as the: "Minions of Menial, the Bosses of the Boring, our Shepherds of Schlep, all the Fools of Facilitation…" Volume 55 (2009) also included a rather cheeky dedication to Jim Dodge, written by Jacob Lehman, to celebrate Jim's departure as Toyon's faculty advisor after 14 years of service.

Volume 55, 2009

Title page of Volume 55, 2009

Class Standout

**Most Eclectic:
Dr. Corey Lee Lewis**

Making a career change as an adult is never easy.

When looking for a person to showcase for the 2000s, there was one person who kept emerging as someone multiple Managing Editors mentioned but seemed to only exist in the pages of Toyon. Dr. Corey Lee Lewis is quite honestly just as spectacular as the journey to find him was. As the Faculty Advisor for Toyon from 2008 to 2014, Corey left teaching at HSU to focus on his writing and build his business not only as an owner of a Taekwondo studio but as a life coach at MindBody Mastery. Corey is Taekwondo Master with a 7th Dan Black Belt and as his bio reads a "licensed master practitioner of neuro-linguistic programming and hypnotherapy." He has published numerous books since he made a career change.

Corey became interested in experiential and holistic education during graduate school. With the staff of Toyon, he utilized a student-centered approach. After a short lecture, the majority of the class time provided space for the students to come up with their own ideas in conversation. Corey remembers that there were always debates among staff members about the aesthetics of a piece. His approach to teaching Toyon was similar to his message as a life coach: you can become anything, become your own champion. When he was advising Toyon, he saw the transition from paper to digital. When he first started as Faculty Advisor, the staff was exclusively taking paper submissions, in which they would make decisions using boards that laid out the issue. By the time he ended his tenure with Toyon, the journal had moved to digital. Corey remembers that Toyon would receive approximately 1,000 poems, 100 stories, and 50 creative nonfiction pieces.

The initial interview with Corey took place in the early days of the COVID-19 pandemic. With the coronavirus, we saw people's engagement in the arts more as a sort of mental refuge from the chaos. With the arts constantly undervalued, under-appreciated but a central part in maintaining sanity, Corey emphasized the idea of democratizing literary spaces to more inclusive. He said, "what the world needs are diverse voices and ideas and solutions…anybody with intelligence and observational skills can tell that the 'white man rule' that we're dealing with right now ain't fucking working—and it has shifted." Corey believes the solutions are out there and they're diverse and coming from small places, like Toyon, with the people on the ground and those doing social justice work. Diverse voices need to be leveraged in the production of knowledge.

One of Corey's favorite memories was the bio written in each volume of Toyon. He recalls that if an author or artist failed to send one, the students would write one for them.

He also remembers particular stories from Toyon about a young man that was in high school at the time coming into his sexual identity. He remembers the tenderness of the scenes in the story and what it allowed readers to understand and see. Corey said, "It's stories like this—this is what literature's for, what stories are for, to help people understand others and create compassion and allies."

The 2010s

2010
- This volume is dedicated to Jim Dodge with the words "O Captain, My Captain."
- This volume is also the first time that Literary Criticism is listed as a genre; guidelines for this genre would appear in 2011.
- This edition also includes the introduction of Russell McGaughey Award in Literary Essay Writing—later to become the English Department Award for Critical Analysis.

2011
- This issue is dedicated to Corey Lee Lewis "whose devotion to environmental advocacy and community well-being continues to inspire those around him."

2012
- This issue is dedicated to Arlene Britt "for her unwavering support, continuous encouragement, and heartwarming smile."
- In this year, the Advisor Award is renamed as the Richard Cortez Day Advisor's Prize in Fiction. The Award Prize was $300 instead of the $100 that honorees of the other active awards receive.

2013
- This volume includes a front matter dedication: "Deadikayted two are Eddytours, wythowt hoom thur wood bee know jernool."

2014
- This volume acknowledges Humboldt State University's Centennial Year.
- This volume is dedicated to Dr. Corey Lewis, with "Flowery Sentiments."
- This also marks the year that *Toyon* went digital: This is the first edition to include a way to submit online (through email).

2015
- Toyon launches its own website in this year. Social Media Icons first appear.
- Online submission upgrade: In this year a Submission Portal is established through the English department website. *Toyon* establishes its own website later that year.

2016

- Toyon officially became multilingual and changes its name to: *Toyon Multilingual Journal of Literature and Art*.
- A new award is established: Multilingual Award for best work in translation or multiple languages (to be later named after Barbara Brinson Curiel at the time of her retirement).
- *Toyon* begins to accept Spoken Word as a genre.
- An Errata slip is needed to correct the omission of Oaxacan poet Guadalupe Angela Ramirez's name from two translated poems.
- The winner of the Toyon Staff Award could not have their art printed in the volume.

2017

- This is the first volume to include a standard copyright page in the front matter.
- This year marks the beginning of the Environmental Studies Award for best work of environmental justice writing or art.
- Inter-sectional politics are showcased throughout the volume.

2018

- In this year, the Fuerza Award for Spoken Word is established, funded by HSU's Lambda Theta Phi Latin Fraternity.

- This is the first time a *Toyon* poem has been published completely in Chinese and translated into English: the piece is titled "Don't Want Regrets" by Rattnak Sokhom.

2019

- The 2019 volume has a special theme: The Movement Issue
- The Multilingual Award renamed to the Barbara Brinson Curiel Multilingual Award after Poet, English & Critical Race and Gender Studies Professor and long-time *Toyon* supporter Barbara Curiel. This is the year of Professor Curiel's retirement.
- This issue has an especially creative design layout with the upper right corner of the volume removed.
- This year hosted the first Spoken Word Event in October—aptly named "A Night of SpOOken Word." QR codes placed in physical book to link to spoken word videos on the website.
- This year is the first time the *Toyon* hosted the annual Campus & Community Dialogue on Race (CDOR) artist dinner for Denice Frohman and Raina León.
- The first Audiobook was created and published with this edition. *Toyon* is possibly the first literary journal that has an audiobook to accompany it.
- The end of the semester saw a new tradition: the "Managing Editor appreciates entire staff" round table speech.
- The co-authors of this book were published in this edition, right after another because of similar subject matter surrounding girls/women/femmes and sexuality.

Volume 55-6, 2010

The 2010s: The Decade of Foresight

The *Toyon* staff throughout the 2010s seemed to have had a crystal ball seeing into the future of *Toyon*, without knowing themselves that they did. The first instance of this literary sorcery can be found in the first issue published in 2010 (volume 56). This edition saw the introduction of Literary Criticism as a submittable genre along with the Russell McGaughey Award in Literary Essay Writing. The first award was given to a literary criticism piece titled "Escaping The Totalitarianism of Everyday Life: Sexual Motivations in Milan Kundera's *The Joke*" by Ansley Clark. Russell McGaughey was a professor in the English Department and a long time contributor to the Toyon. Although volume 56 introduced literary criticism as genre in 2010 the guidelines for the genre weren't published until 2011. This issue was dedicated to Jim Dodge with the inscription "O Captain, My Captain" on the title page.

From 2011 to 2014, each edition was creatively dedicated to a person(s) that had an impact on the staff on each year. Corey Lee Lewis, who was an English Professor and Faculty Advisor for *Toyon*, on many occasions received a dedication for his "...devotion to environmental advocacy and community well-being [that] continues to inspire those around him," as written in Volume 57 (2011). The next year, Arlene Britt, an English Department Administrator, received high praise "for her unwavering support,

Volume 55-6, 2010

continuous encouragement, and heart warming smile." That same volume (58) saw the renaming of the Advisor's Award to the Richard Cortez Day Advisor's Prize in Fiction which, at the time, awarded the winner $300 unlike the $100 prize the other awards offered. The staff of volume 59 had a sense of humor in their dedication to the Editor, they joked that this book was "Deadikayted two are Eddytours, wythowt hoom thur wood bee know jernool." While Corey Lee Lewis was again recognized with "Flowery Sentiments" in volume 60.

Volume 58, 2012

Volume 59, 2013

The second half of the 2010s saw *Toyon* integrate itself into the digital world. Volume 60 (2014) was the first time that submissions were collected online, originally through a *Toyon* gmail account. It is safe to assume that the amount of submissions received in the gmail account was overwhelming enough for the English Department to set up a submission portal for Toyon the next year. Social media icons for the English Department's Facebook and Twitter were printed in volume 61 (2015). In 2016 (volume 62), *Toyon* rolled out its own website autonomous from the English Department, and offered Spoken Word an official genre. *Toyon* was always involved with Spoken Word as far back as the 70s, but it wasn't until volume 62 that it became emphasized in the call for submissions. Since the creation of *Toyon*'s unique website, *Toyon* is now read in 108 countries across six continents. (The penguins don't have access to a stable Wi-Fi connection in Antarctica.)

Toyon saw more growth beyond just digital integration in 2016. *Toyon* changed its subtitle to *Toyon Multilingual Journal of Literature and Art* as well as the addition of the Multilingual Award for best work in translation or multiple languages. Volume 62 became the second volume to include an Errata from the staff typed on "fancier" paper found somewhere between the pages, they wrote:

Volume 60, 2014

> **"Published in this issue are two poems English translations of poems originally written in Spanish by poet Guadalupe Ángela Ramirez, translated by Kirk Alvaro Lua. Ramirez's name was mistakenly left out of the original printing of the issue. The Toyon Staff apologizes for this oversight."**

Volume 61, 2015

Volume 62, 2016

To add to the quirkiness of the volume, the winner of the Toyon Staff Award, "Emociones Mixtas" by Ashley Underwood has a note from the staff placed on an artless page that states: "This year's Toyon Staff Award Winner for best work of visual art cannot appear in the journal. However, the Toyon staff wishes to acknowledge the work of artist Ashley Underwood here."

Volume 63 in 2017 produced its own expansion of *Toyon*. Before this issue, *Toyon* had never produced a copyright page that solidified it as its own independent literary journal. Glossy, high resolution paper was used to showcase the art of this edition in full color; the signature was placed in the middle of the book. This edition produced a lot of changes to the awards that were offered, they are as follows:

- The start of the Environmental Studies Award for best work of environmental justice writing or art whose first winner was "The Watchers of the Water" by Luke T. McCarthy.
- The beginning and ending of the Department of World Languages and Cultures Trilingual Poetry Award which had three winners-(1st) "Reganos" by Ihovanna Huezo, (2nd) "Ni de aquí ni de allá" by Jessica Melgoza, (3rd) "Who I Am" by Andrea C. Curtade.
- Lastly, the renaming of the English Department Award and Toyon Multilingual Award.

Volume 63, 2017

In true *Toyon* fashion, this volume was very political since it followed immediately after the 2016 election of Donald Trump as President. There was a particular theme of interrogating identity politics that can be found across all genres. In these pages Latinx identities are grappled with in Spanish and English. Everything from police violence to food politics are living within these pages. Like the writings found after the Vietnam War in the 50s, the artists and authors of *Toyon* were enmeshed with the reality of changing the world.

The 2018 volume of Toyon (64) became slightly infamous for its "Toyon Green" cover. Besides its interesting shade of green, this volume introduced the Fuerza Award for Spoken Word. The gentlemen of the Lambda Theta Phi Latin Fraternity, Inc at HSU generously fund this award to "promote the cultural significance of oral interpretations and to encourage

Volume 64, 2018

writers to think of their work beyond the page. The award name is drawn from Lambda Theta Phi's motto: *En la unión está la fuerza (In unity there is strength)*.

The 2018 volume is noteworthy for several reasons. Within the pages of this volume is a poem named "Don't Want Regrets" by Rattnak Sokhom. It

Volume 64 staff members working in the computer lab

Volume 65, 2019

is the first poem published in *Toyon* that is completely in Chinese and translated into English. It's work like "Don't Want Regrets" that drives *Toyon*'s mission in celebrating multilingualism in the literary world.

This decade concludes with a flare created only by those who pour their love and care into the creation of *Toyon*. The 65th anniversary volume in 2019 was the biggest and brightest edition to date. In this "Movement Issue," the staff thought this theme would be fitting for the current political climate. At this time the staff become more aware of the internment camps that were imprisoning immigrants and people who are undocumented, specifically those of Latinx identity. The staff wanted to know what others would make of the theme centered around movement and received some phenomenal pieces, as expected. The theme was taken a step further during the production phase of creating this volume. Some pages are typeset in a landscape position with arrows to direct the reader, creating its own form of movement. This particular staff voted to have a corner cut off the entire book, not only for the aesthetic but to set the text to interact with the missing corner. There is not another literary journal housed on a University campus that literally cuts corners, making *Toyon* unique.

Beyond the physical edition of *Toyon*, the staff participated in and created events that later became annual events hosted by *Toyon*. The first annual SpOOken Word event was held in the Fulkerson Recital Hall at HSU. This Halloween-themed event was the idea of the Spoken Word and web team which included that year's archivist. The event was attended by students and local community members. This event was followed by another spoken word event that was in collaboration with CDOR or Campus & Community Dialogue on Race. CDOR is "an annual event at Humboldt State University that invites students, staff, faculty, administrators, and community members to present and attend programs that relate to racial justice and its intersections with all forms of oppression and resistance." CDOR agreed to let *Toyon* host the Artist Dinner for Keynote presenters every year. *Toyon* hosted both spoken word artist and educator, Denice Frohman as well as the English Department's visiting writer, Dr. Raina J.León. Both artists were entertained with the beautiful spoken word performances by the students and community members in attendance.

Detail of the Volume 65 corner cut

The 65th edition continued to deliver unprecedented growth and creativity. *Toyon* created its first audiobook to accompany the volume. This very well might be the first and only literary journal in general to have an audiobook attached to it. The staff of *Toyon* has always been committed to making *Toyon a*ccessible. By creating an audiobook, not only did they bridge a gap in the accessibility of the journal but also introduced *Toyon* to a whole new audience.

The 2010s concluded with the same foresight that it began with. The Managing Editor of volume 65, Anthony Alonzo-Pereira, didn't know that the tradition of giving an appreciation to each staff member at the end of the semester would be upheld by the next Managing Editor. Neither of the authors of this very book knew that consequently getting published right next to each other in volume 65 would lead to them co-authoring a book about the legacy of *Toyon*. The students of *Toyon* have created pure magic in the last 65 years, but there is still more to come.

Class Standout

Modest Visionary: Dr. Janelle Adsit

Dr. Janelle Adsit was surprised with an interview to be the 2010s Class Standout only because she does not favor the spotlight and proudly attributes all the beautiful things that happened in her tenure as Faculty Advisor from 2015 to 2020 to the students she has worked with over the years. Janelle has a long history with equity work starting as early as her undergraduate career with her work with Habitat for Humanity to her recent volunteer work in palliative care. She notes that her practice as an ally is a continuous journey and possibly the reason she seldom sleeps. She feels a tremendous responsibility to show up for all of her students in a way that is affirming and transforms the educational institutions that she's a part of to deconstruct inequitable practices in the academy.

When Janelle accepted the job offer from the English Department in 2015, *Toyon* was just beginning to make its transition to the digital world. In her early stages of the interview process, Janelle recalls a lunch with Dr. Barbara Curiel and Jim Dodge discussing how they envisioned the future of *Toyon* to move into a more bilingual direction in order to best represent the students in the English Department. She was hired to bring the journal online to increase accessibility and complement the print journal. She envisioned a multi-modal journal that now includes a dynamic spoken word division and an audiobook. The goal was to begin to "build a more inclusive and social justice-oriented magazine that would enable transnational and transcultural exchange within the pages of the journal." Janelle notes *Toyon* far surpasses what she envisioned originally and it is due to the ingenuity and brilliance of the staff.

Her informal beginning with publishing started with her dad who would write down things she would say and create booklets that he would then gift to her as a child. Janelle thought it was so powerful that someone cared enough about her words to put it in a book that she began the journey of doing the same for others. Her mom was also a librarian for a short amount of time so books were always around her. For all of you that have attended a release party since 2015 know that "Mama Toyon" (Janelle's mother) is an absolute joy and the original Modest Visionary. Janelle began her formal journey with publishing as an undergrad at Colorado State University as the Poetry Editor at their literary magazine which was named with just a single letter "A" at the time. She also worked in various trade publications, yet she credits all she knows about publishing to a master's internship at the *Colorado Review* and being taught by Stephanie G'Schwind, the Faculty Advisor who ran the Center of Literary Publishing at Colorado State.

Janelle views the staff of *Toyon* as change makers in the publishing industry – who will become cultural producers and fight the inequalities that exist in the industry with radical transformation. To create this change, every aspect of the publishing process needs to be led by people in the room with diverse perspectives to shift the conversations and center social justice as a normative practice. People who understand what's at stake can create a world in which disposability is no longer the "business as usual" politics. Those who have been part of *Toyon* work tirelessly to create a microcosm that can be applied to the industry at large.

Some of Janelle's favorite memories from *Toyon* are having the privilege of learning from her staff and students that she's worked with the last couple of years. The annual book release celebration is one of her favorite events. The Fall 2018 staff gifted her a squirrel ornament after she confessed that during a job interview she panicked when asked what type of animal she most resembles and she picked a squirrel. It's those small things that continue to bring her joy. Janelle also cherishes the tradition of staff members at the end of the semester going around and sharing appreciation for each individual staff member. It's the love and kindness that is shared within the *Toyon* and given freely amongst those who support the journal that proves that Janelle's vision has quickly become a reality.

Adsit (center front) with the Volume 64 staff

TOYON LORE

About A Published Piece Called 'Toy-On It!'

In 2019 Toyon published a piece like no other, "Toy-On It!" It wasn't the vulgar language which set the piece apart, nor the constant references to sex, drugs, and mahogany furniture. Instead, in an act of sweet narcissism, it became the first piece published by *Toyon* about *Toyon*. But then again, if Toyon writing about Toyon is wrong, why the heck are you reading this book? Can I swear? I sure frigging hope so. And I sure hope my editor doesn't replace all the curse words with PG replacements.

"Toy-On It" was also unique for its comedic tone, especially in a magazine with serious issues. Pun intended. Some felt the piece made fun of Toyon while others believed it celebrated the publication. This disagreement led to a feud between the two camps and a spate of duels broke out in the editorial offices as sword met sword and blood met blood. Eventually the piece was published and only one question remained, "Who the fork wrote it?" No one was sure, but it was my job to find out.

The writer was listed as Glenage DeRyan, but no person of that name existed ever, and his author's bio was short, vague, and ultimately useless as the male nipple. "Glenage DeRyan is the name of a person who goes to HSU It's totally not Raymond Carver though, who's still super dead." The bio told me two things, I could eliminate Raymond Carver from my search and Glenage DeRyan had missed a period. Pun not intended this time.

Some people thought Glenage DeRyan was me, Gary Dean Engle, just because our names are perfect anagrams for each other. If only it were true, my search would have been over. Instead I poured through old volumes of Toyon, looking for a clue. Finally, I found one, an old editor, Ryan Gene Gadel, whose name was yet another perfect anagram. Sure, my anagrammed name was a coincidence, but as my grandfather always said, "two coincidences are either fate or Satan." I was betting on fate.

I tracked down Mr. Gadel to his Eureka Victorian. He was not as I expected. He had long legs but a perfectly round torso, not a corner to him. His remaining hair was tinged with gray, but his Van Dyke beard was a violent shade of aqua-maroon.

I wasted no time, "Are you Glenage DeRyan, author of 'Toy-On It?'"
"Yes," he said.
"Why did you write it? Why did you want to make fun of Toyon."
Mr. DeRyan/ Gadel paused, and said, simply, "I liked it... Goodbye." Then he slammed the door in my face.

I do not know what Glenage DeRyan meant, or why he wrote the piece. But I have a guess. Nothing is sacrosanct, not even the things we love, and to truly appreciate and understand something, you have to be able to laugh at it.

Also, seriously I'm not Glenage DeRyan, stop fracking saying I am.

-Gary Dean Engle, July 2019

Gary Dean Engle and cohort Heather Rumsey recording the Toyon Audiobook, 2019

TOYON LORE

An Unlikely Mascot: Nic Cage

In 2018 book designer, Sarah Godlin purchased a poster of actor Nicolas Cage reading Siddhartha upside down for an interactive advertisement promoting the Toyon and the class. Cage is one of the most ubiquitous actors of a generation, but his appearance on the *Toyon* bulletin board was intended as a silly joke. *Toyon* staff maintained a collaborative writing space on our designated bulletin board on the second floor of Founder's Hall to advertise for the magazine and to engage with the student body. He was originally posted with the question, "What's your favorite book?"

Despite how much the staff loved the Nic Cage mascot, they did not foresee the draw of Nic Cage and he was unceremoniously stolen from the bulletin board with no trace of a suspect. Staff beseeched students to return Nic, no questions asked, but were rebuffed and instead subject to nasty barbs traded back and forth, via bulletin board, between *Toyon* staff and whoever is assumed to be the culprit. Nic Cage was never recovered. Undeterred, the *Toyon* staff continued to engage students via the bulletin board despite the pitfalls of open and unmoderated

Georges Biard, Creative Commons license

discussion. Many on the spot redactions and edits have been made to maintain the integrity of the *Toyon* bulletin board. In 2019, to celebrate the release of volume 65, the Toyon staff created the "Where's Nic?" coloring and activity book that was available at the release party event. While Nic's era may have ended too soon, the legacy is sure to live on as the creative and fun spirit of the Toyon staff, which has at least one Nic Cage coffee cup in the staff lounge.

Founder's Hall bulletin board: The scene of the crime

Nic Cage continues on in this display

The 2020s

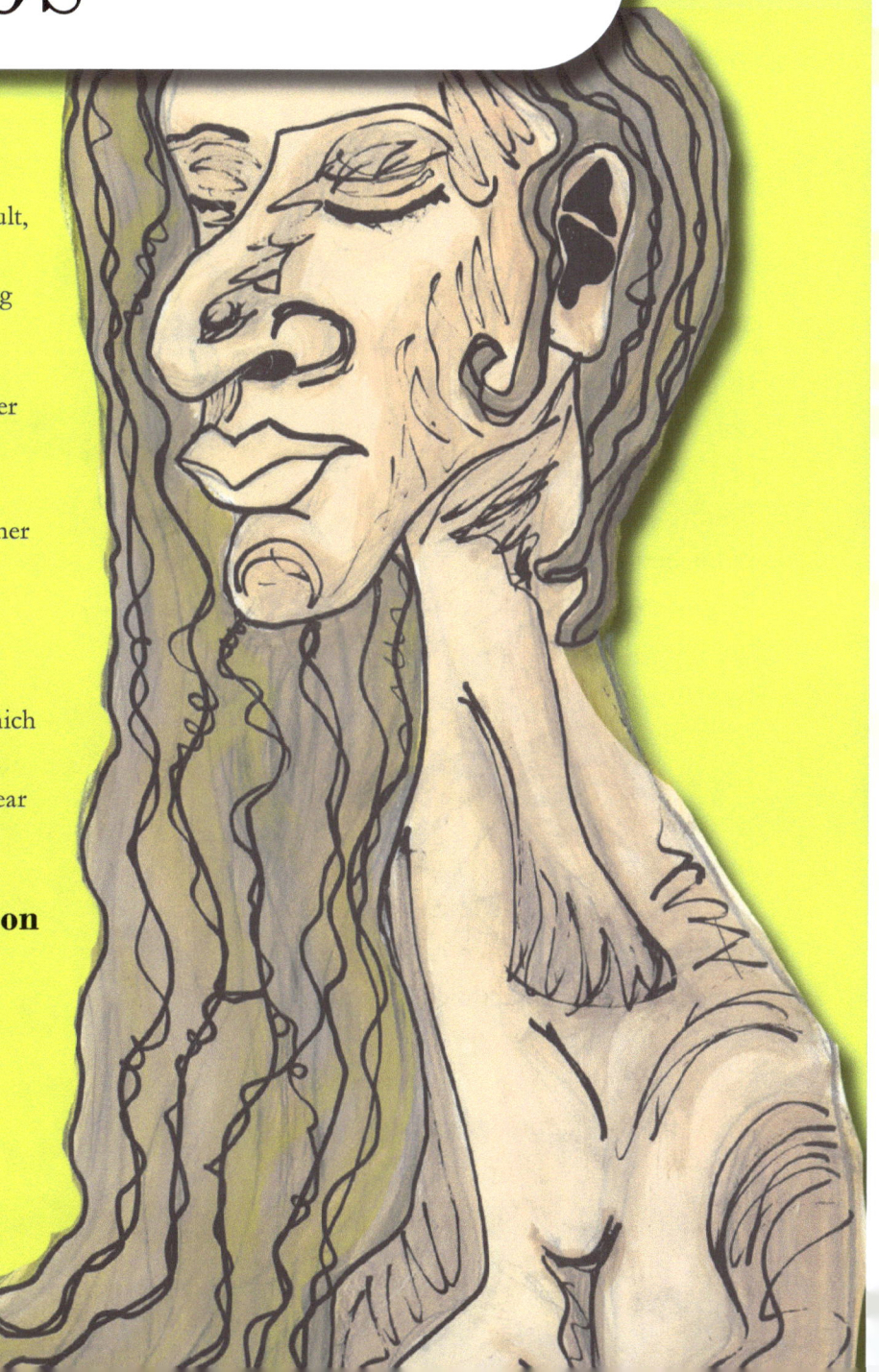

2020
- Power Blackouts due to California wildfires made compiling the 2020 Taboo issue difficult, but it was done!
- COVID 19 restrictions close campus, making the Toyon a distance education class.
- The class changed faculty advisors. Marcos Hernandez stepped into Janelle Adsit's former role.

2021
- The latest issue, Volume 67, includes the corner cut.
- The Toyon operated 100% online for both semesters while building Volume 67.
- The magazine received funding from HSU's office of Diversity, Equity, and Inclusion, which allowed the hire of two translators.
- This year there were submissions which appear in three different languages.

Additional writing by Joshua Lamason

The 2020s: Unexpected Beginnings

The magic of Toyon continued into the beginning of the new decade, with some unexpected wielding no one saw coming. It began in Fall with the 2019-2020 staff, excited to create volume 66 with a theme of "exploring the taboo," began experiencing numerous blackouts which took some in-class time away from the staff. Spring offered a short reprieve from the semester before only to hear the news of the passing of Oaxacan poet Guadalupe Ángela Ramirez. Guadalupe Ángela, who was published in previous issues of *Toyon*, was to give a poetry reading at HSU but passed the weekend before. She is remembered for her tremendous contribution to Mexican poetry, as an avid advocate for women, and as a long-cherished supporter of Toyon. Spring also brought news of the early stages of the Covid-19 global pandemic and moved the release party to the virtual sphere. A global pandemic did not stop the 2020-2021 staff from producing a more inclusive multilingual edition for volume 67 or from celebrating the new Faculty Advisor Marcos Hernandez. Those

Volume 66, 2020

who have worked on *Toyon* know a great deal about resilience, regardless of time or place *Toyon* is produced, the staff has continuously overcome the odds. Just because the start was rocky does not mean that *Toyon Multilingual Literary Magazine* is going to run out of magic anytime soon.

The back, spine and middle of Volume 67. This is the way the file is presented to the printer. The black triangles indicates where the cuts will be made.

Making Toyon

From Acquisitions to Release

A Brief Timeline of Volume 65, The Movement Issue

1. Advertising and Submissions

a.   The cycle of publishing never really stops for an ongoing publication but obviously we need submissions to create a whole magazine, so that's where the cycle begins. Toyon has a set submission deadline of September 30 but the date has fluctuated as much as the magazine throughout history. Having a set deadline every year helps us ground the Toyon and build a class around it. During this part of the cycle the Fall semester starts and roles of the masthead are established. With that comes the production of various flyers. The staff also works to establish web and social media campaigns, and schedule times and places to table and advertise the current issue of Toyon along with putting out the Call for Submissions.

b.   The Call for Submissions is out for Toyon all year round. Which side of September 30 a submission is received determines when the piece will be considered. Most of our submissions come from students and the university community, so the bulk of submissions for a current issue come in September, up until the deadline. The scope and reach of our submission process depends largely on the student editors: how and where they advertise.

The volume 65 staff was very committed to getting as many submissions as we could. The social media team went to Arts!Alive in Eureka and Arcata. The spoken word team went to poetry events around town every week, like Word Humboldt @ Northtown Coffee and The Humboldt Poetry Show @ The Siren's Song Tavern.

2. Selection: Choosing What Goes In and What Stays Out

a.   After September 30th, the fun begins. Staffers and editors are assigned a genre and a collection of submissions; the reading and rating begins. Before reading commences the team spends some time determining what makes something worthy of being in Toyon. A rubric is created and agreed upon. All of October is spent reading submissions and figuring out what is going to end up in the book. This is a lengthy and tedious process.

Volume 65 had over 200 submissions! We were all pretty excited to see and read all the submissions.

b.   This part of the process is exciting but stressful. There is a lot of pressure to fill an entire volume of Toyon. October is also the time of midterms in other classes because it is the middle of the Fall semester. After reading and sending the rankings, editors meet and determine the final pieces based on which pieces scored highest. The team decides together the approximate ratio each genre will take up in the finished book. There are more poetry submissions than fiction, generally, but prose genres are longer and take up more space. Section editors meet after every class session in late October to narrow down selections. By November there is a rough idea of what will be included in the next volume and emphasis shifts to the design of the book, typesetting, and editing.

Poetry editors for the Movement Issue were torn by so many great pieces and only about 7 slots allotted. It wasn't until a whole staff meeting that they realized that they could fight for more poetry slots if there were more poems of worth.

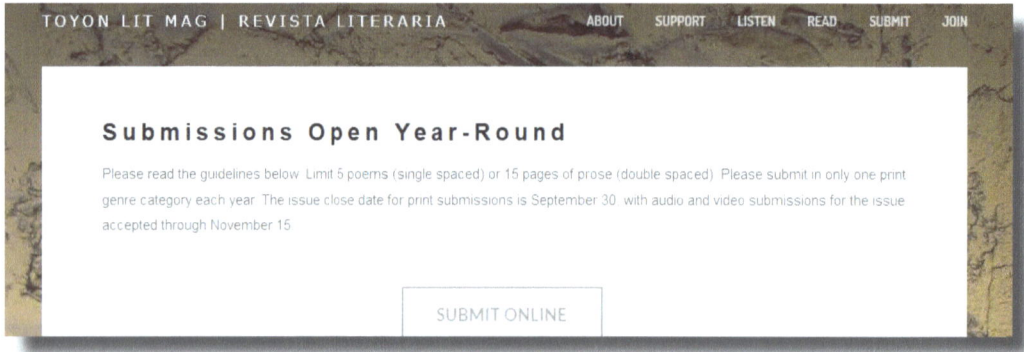

3. Copy Editing, Style, and Design

a.	By the end of November (or before Thanksgiving break, hopefully) there is a rough version of the book called the copy version, or the book before it is copy edited. The copy-editing stage is where the guts of the book are edited for grammar, clarity and conciseness. This is also the stage in which any fact-checking, citations, and copyrights come into play. It is important to get permission from creators when editing pieces for clarity or fact-checking.

b.	Ultimately, Toyon is the vessel for several authors and artists' work; it is the authors' work solely. Toyon only has the rights to print in this edition. Editors always strive to let authors and artists have as much control over their piece as possible, however, formatting issues cause editors to have to take out parts of text.

Our literary criticism editors used QR codes, or web-based scannable codes that let the reader download the longer piece, for their section. Critical pieces are often longer than creative pieces and usually harder to cut information from.

c.	Throughout October the production team, in addition to assisting in rating submissions, works on designing a color palette, picking fonts, and creating a visual guide for the final book; this is related to the style guide for the magazine, but is specific to the issue. Toyon changes the cover style often, unlike other literary magazines that keep consistent cover templates. On trend with the ebb and flow of new student editors, the Toyon takes shape based on the whims of the student editors.

Volume 65 was labeled the "movement issue" with the tagline "everything moves" and we anticipated a wide variation and interpretation of this theme. Our design team used the idea of human foot traffic, literal movement, in the cover design. Unique to the design was the cut upper right corner making Toyon a polygon instead of a standard rectangle. The design dares the reader to view the book itself as a piece of art, a subversion of traditional book and page layout.

4. Proofreading

a. Everyone in the team lends a hand in "proofing" the volume before the final proof is sent to the printers. In 2018, copy editor Max Hosford, created the first style guide for Toyon. Most major publications, such as The New York Times and Rolling Stone Magazine, have a set of style guidelines. These are the rules of style throughout all issues and articles in a publication, setting not only font size and margins, but punctuation rules, preferred spellings, and how to format abbreviations. Many magazines and newspapers follow Chicago or APA formats. Our Toyon's style guide is based on Chicago.

b. Using the style guide created for Toyon, the staff combs the copy of the guts for specific errors and typos. One way this is accomplished is to assign checkers for specific elements. For example, a person is assigned to check for numbers throughout the copy assuring that the style guide for written numerals is followed. As always, original authors have final say over how their piece is formatted in the final book.

c. Proofing is the last step before approving the book to be printed. In 2019, Toyon utilized the on-campus printing capabilities from Marketing and Communications (MARCOM) to publish the physical book from Humboldt State University Library Press. In the past, Toyon has utilized local small presses in the community.

d. Proofing is also the last section of English 460 before the Fall semester ends. Many of the students who took the class in the Fall will return for the Spring section, but those who still have a role to play in the next half of production usually volunteer their time to the magazine, though not always through course enrollment.

5. Marketing

a.   The Spring semester opens with marketing, not unlike the call for submissions, but now outreach focuses on planning the release party and advertising for the upcoming publication. While Toyon is not typically sold for a fee, we have in the past offered Toyon for sale at local bookstores like Northtown Books in Arcata and Booklegger in Eureka. It is reliant on the budget and the decision of the outreach and editorial teams how disbursement of the magazine should be dealt with.

We were ambitious in what Toyon could accomplish with additional grants and funding. The spoken word team took on the recording of an audiobook of Toyon volume 65 (unheard of for student-run undergraduate publications) as well as video recordings of spoken word poems.

b.   Significant attention is paid to maximizing the accessibility of Toyon—having not only audio versions, but also ensuring the digital copy is optimized for screen readers used by hearing impaired readers. The Toyon website is continually being updated to be as accessible as possible taking into account readability, translation, screen-reading optimization, and easy-to-see color schemes.

No one gave us the direction to make the book so accessible. When as a staff we spoke of inclusion, we really took it to heart and we made sure Volume 65 was available on more platforms than ever before. All pieces are available digitally from Humboldt Digital Commons, through the magazine app Issuu, and as an audiobook format on Youtube and SoundCloud.

6. Release Party

a.   Everyone has a hand in the release party. Janelle (as faculty advisor) booked the Kate Buchanan room months in advance for March to align with the spring course schedule. But before we can unload Costco snacks and set up chairs, we spend a few weeks planning how we want to present our new baby to the world.

b.   The outreach team continues to advertise the upcoming party and the publication of the Toyon. A separate party planning team plans for entertainment, budget for snacks and refreshments, and selects an emcee

Everyone unanimously picked Dean Engle to be emcee because if you know him you know it's the role he was born to play. Mireille Roman also was elected as emcee, presenting a Spanish-language version of the evening's events.

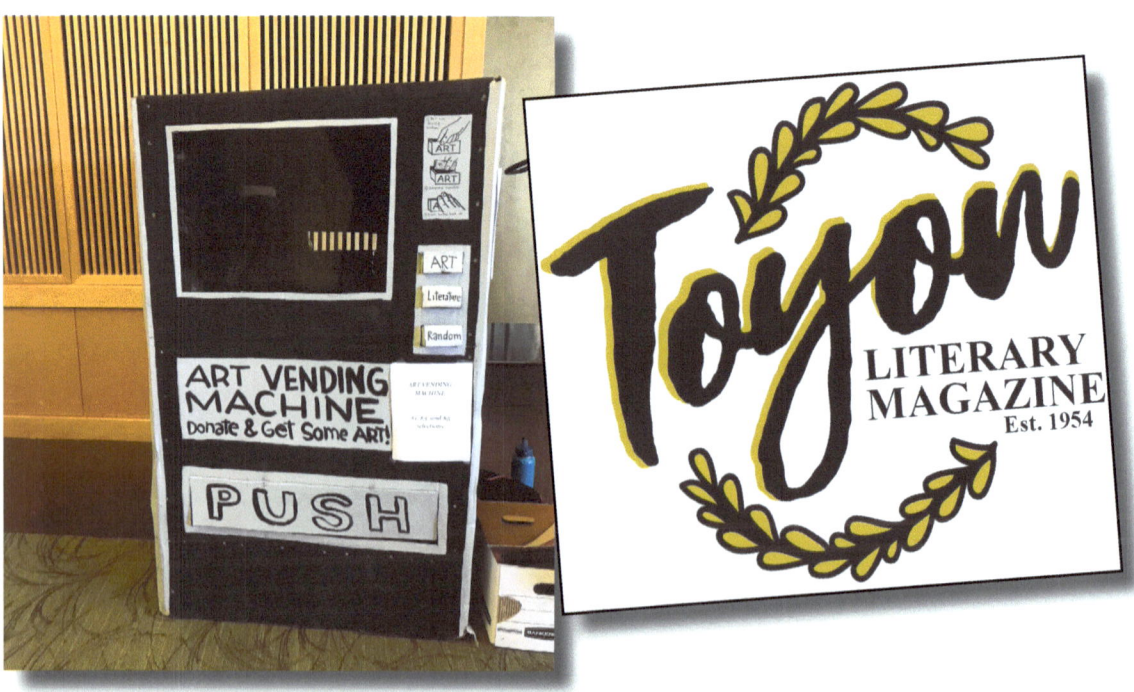

c.   Our swag guru designs new stickers and a variety of other fun party favors with Toyon's name on it, old-school style. Embracing the true DIY-spirit of the greater Humboldt area, our stickers come right out of our office printer and then are stuck to notebooks, pencils, and seed packets.

When the day of the party finally came, we were ready, armed with stickers, handmade Toyon hand-stamps and beautifully silkscreened Toyon shirts made by local artists at Bodega in Eureka. It was satisfying to see our work come to life.

d.   After several months of running around and not feeling like you know what you're doing, the book is finally printed! A few days later, the audiobook goes live, as do the print-on-demand options via Amazon's Kindle Direct Publishing service. The release party is a chance for the editorial staff to celebrate and show off the hard work put in. It's also how we share Toyon with the community. Often for the first time, the Toyon staff is meeting the writers, poets, and artists who submitted their work.

e.   Volume 65 beginning to end!

Notes from the Authors

From Asha Galindo

The opportunity to write *Toyon*'s history was like any other opportunity that came along during my tenure as a student editor of *Toyon*: it was brought up once in class as an idea, I raised my hand, and three months later I was sitting across from our faculty advisor Janelle Adsit, Kyle Morgan from HSU Press, Carly Marino and Louis Knecht from Special Collections, and Erika Andrews, and we were discussing timelines and deadlines. We were given a lot of freedom to create our vision of *Toyon* history, and figuring out what counts was really up to us. It wasn't unlike going into the production cycle with little knowledge of my position, but I learned then by diving in feet first and basically trying things out. That is really the crux of working on *Toyon*, isn't it?

It was clear the first time I began looking at the archived volumes that *Toyon* was completely reinvented every year. Each issue forms a little picture. Sometimes it's a picture of the decade or the political climate. Often, it's a snapshot of the editors: what they valued about literature and art, if they had an agenda, if they were funny or serious, if they ran out of money. The most exciting part of taking on the project of writing *Toyon*'s history was how the picture was different every year. It was always *Toyon*. It always contained what was agreed to be the best submissions that year. There was usually some kind of masthead. If I was lucky there was an editor's letter, and maybe contributor bios, something to tell me about the people who made it.

Author Notes

The other thing that stuck out was how professional each issue looked, as an example of student work. I could reasonably expect this in the modern era where technology makes so many things possible in desktop publishing, but I was struck by how good *Toyon* issues looked in the 1960s and 1970s, in the days when editors were laying out the pages by hand or hand-typing the copy.

The idiosyncrasies of the different editorial boards over the years led me to my biggest conclusion of the entire project: this is our story. *Toyon* is important for being a platform for student literary endeavors, but as a student-run journal, it's about the creation as much as it's about the works within it. There is an entire story unfolding during the production cycle of *Toyon*. That's the story I tried to keep in mind when I was working on this book. I both wanted to interpret the archives and make sure I was keeping track of the history as it's happening.

In Spring 2019 on the last day of English 461, we passed our new copies of Volume 65 around the room, autographing them for each other. Maybe it was because this staff had a lot of graduating seniors, but *Toyon* 65 was our yearbook. We wrote little notes to each other about how privileged we were to work together, how we're going to rule the world, and how we all better hire each other one day.

When I started working on *Toyon: 65 Years of Student Driven Publishing* I realized that a yearbook was a good metaphor for the project. *Toyon* is our chance to make our mark on the world, to be a part of the history of HSU, the English department, and a part of a literary tradition.

Putting together an issue of *Toyon* isn't a formula that you can follow. There are some basic instructions about when submissions are due, what tasks have to happen, etc. But at the end of the day *Toyon* happens if you want it to. The outcome of the journal is what you put into it initially. If you work hard at producing something you believe in, you will produce something great. That is how I approached writing this book.

Asha Galindo
April 2020

From Erika Andrews

I was a transfer student when I came to HSU, so I had the plan of making the most of college before my FASFA ran out. With righteous indignation, I started my time with *Toyon* as the Assistant Managing Editor in Fall 2018, after professing to Dr. Janelle Adsit my ambition of wanting to be Managing Editor. She suggested the Assistant Managing Editor position—a three-semester commitment that would ultimately end in the job I wanted. As Assisting Managing Editor, with the help of my team, we were able to get 10x the amount of spoken word submissions than the previous year and start an annual spoken word event that still goes on until this day. As Managing Editor, I got to lead and teach the entire Toyon Staff. I say this to remind you all that nothing in Toyon happens without the support of the staff. My ambition was only realized because I was supported by every single person in Toyon one way or another. I am truly grateful to each and every one of you for trusting me with our joint vision. It's not every day that a queer, black kid gets to shine so unapologetically.

I got this idea in community college that I was going to write and publish a book by the age of 23. I forgot it until I was finishing up my first book—*Y.E.S.: 50 Years of Community Building*—at the age of 23. This book in your hands was created to do what that book did, tell the history of the organization, and celebrate the people who have been a part of it. I was lucky enough to have Asha as a co-author this time and be a person who "knows" *Toyon*. We wanted to write this book to serve as a learning tool for future *Toyon* staff so they could understand that they too are a part of the living history of *Toyon*.

Author Notes

This book is particularly important to me because as a first-generation college student with so many intersectional identities that are deemed marginalized, I know how important for people who look like me to see that this is possible. We all know how white, ablest and elitist publishing as an industry is. It brings me great joy that my sheer existence challenges that status quo. I was able to experience what intentional steps towards a more just literary process look like and with some of the most inspirational people I have ever gotten the pleasure of meeting.

With that being said, I would like to thank the Spoken Word, Web Design, and Archive team—the first small team that I got to work with—for always being open to my boundless ambition and making the vision come true. Thank you, Mireille Roman and Theresa Lopez for always getting it with a simple look since Dr. Stacey's class. I have seen both of you grow into amazing human beings and I am so proud and inspired by you both every day. Thank you Asha Galindo for being a brilliant writer and keeping me on my toes. Thank you Sarah Godlin for being patient with me as I finished this book. Thank you Kyle Morgan and HSU Press for all your help and endless smiles. Lastly, thank you Dr. Janelle Adsit for being one of the best professors and mentors a small human like myself can wish for.

If there is a will, you will always find your way and hopefully not alone. I hope your wildest dreams come true and bring you freedom.

Until the next time,

Erika Andrews
February 2021

People of Toyon

To honor all the work of Toyon editors throughout the last 66 years, here are the names of staff and advisors beginning in 1954

1954
Editors: Frances Stark, Robert Pepper, Beverly Dahlen, Bruce Campbell, Craig Stark
Advisor: Giles Sinclair

1956
Editors: Joy Branaman, Erlene Hemenway, Barbara Johnson

1957
Staff: Tony Vasquez, Ronald Sells, Todd Collins, Roberta Ellis, Dathene Gammon, Garth Stull, Gabriel Carranco, Alan Hendrickson
Advisor: Ralph Samuelson

1958
Editor-in-chief: Todd Collins
Staff: Ronald Sells, Dathene Stanley
Cover Design: Todd Collins
Faculty Advisor: Ralph Samuelson

1959
Editor-in-chief: Janis Williams
Staff: Tony Doyle, Bruce Paige, Karl Harber
Cover Design: Joe Romero
Faculty Advisor: Ralph Samuelson

1960
Editors: Patrick and Carol Quinn
Faculty Advisor: Robert Brant

1961
Editor: Ken Gatlin
Staff: Marie Aylward, Dick Turner, Bill Livingston
Cover Design: Gordon Hill
Faculty Advisor: R.C. Day

1962
Volume 8, Number 1
Editors: Anna M. Davis and Peg Falkenberg
Nameplate Design: Peg Falkenberg

1962 – Volume 8, Number 2
Editor: Linda Dungan

1963
Editor: Raymond Carver
Staff: Patti Anderson,
Derrald Vaughn
Cover Design: Robert Lopez
Advisor: R.C. Day

1964
Editor: Barbara Flora
Staff: Sarah Toon
Cover Design: D. Ronk,
Ron Stammer
Faculty Advisor: R.C. Day

1965
Editor: Don Ronk
Assistant Editor: Sarah Toon
Art Editor: Diane Epifani
Staff: Eugene Brundin,
W.D. Skiles
Cover Design: Nelson Wheeler
Faculty Advisor:
Harold Bragen

1966
Editor: Eugene G. Brundin
Assistant Editor:
Cheryl Langston
Staff: Linda McCauley, Michael
Nilan, Nancy Shirk,
J. W. Twibell
Faculty Advisor:
Harold Bragen
Art Advisor: William Thonson

1967
General Editor:
Cheryl Langston
Copy Editors: Nancy Shirk,
Eugene Brundin
Art Editor:
Jane Marie Cleveland
Advisor: Harold Bragen
Art Advisor: William Thonson
Cover Design: Ron Metzler

1968
Editor: Joan Hoffman
Assistant Editor:
Jerry Nusbaum
Staff: Leah Taylor,
Steven Phipps
Advisor: Harold Bragen
Cover Design and Line
Drawings: Lewis Call

1969
General Editors: Steven
Phipps, Joseph Fusco
Photo Consultant:
Thomas Cooper
Cover Photo: Dale McKinnon

1970
Editor: Richard May
Design & Production:
R. J. Moroni
Staff: Douglas Beauchamp
Cover: R.J. Moroni (with Susan
Herman drawing on back
cover)

1971
Editor In Chief:
Mike McCamman
Art Editor: Mark Ivan
Staff: Marty Beidler, Stephen
Fountain, Scott Gilroy, Marcia
Myasaki, Peter Pennekamp,
Elizabeth Petty, Sandra Shand,
Katy Spear, Gail Williams
Faculty Advisors:
Ralph Samuelson and
John B. Dalsant

Past Toyon Staff

Faculty Consultants: Giles Sinclair, William Honsa, E. L. Squires, Victor Fascio, William Thonson

1972
Editor: Webb Bauer
Manuscript Editor: George Justice
Art Director: Dale Smith

1973
Editor: Kristen Atkinson
Publicity: Shirley Wible
Faculty Advisors: Merton Harris, Terry Clarke

1974
Editor: Kristen Suzanne Atkinson
Art Editor: Shirley Wible
Advisor: Merton Harris

1975
Editors: Cynthia Mossman, Debra Winnikoff
Faculty Advisor: Jim Dodge
Cover Painting: Larry Gray

1976
Editors: Arrietta Chakos, Rick Hibbard
Faculty Advisor: Jim Dodge

1977
Editors: L. D. Engdahl, Lachlin Loud, Steven J. Skelley
Faculty Advisor: Jim Dodge
Cover: Pamela Kirk, *Les Mystérieuses*

1978
Editors: Tim Badger, Clifford Hunt
Contributing Editors: Doug Michele, K.A. McCord, Jack Skelley, Peter Shock, Mark Savage, Jack Herron
Managing Editor: Anne Uetz
Faculty Advisor: Maura Stanton

1979
Editors: Eris Hawley Slack, D.R. Laux, Brooke Thacker
Art Editor: Lorinda Ruddiman
Graphics Advisor: William Thonson
Technical Assistants: Lori Griffith, Lon Porter
Faculty Advisor: Jayne Anne Phillips

1980
Editor: Lon Porter
Assistant Editor: Mary Ellen Johnson
Technical Assistant: Peter Farley
Cover: H.S.U. Media Center

1981
Editor: Mary Ellen Johnson
Assistant Editor: Rod Sanborn
Editorial and Technical Assistants: Peter Farley, Christopher Davis, George Taylor
Faculty Advisor: James Galvin
Cover Design: HSU Media Graphics

1982
Editor: Rod Sanborn
Assistant Editor: David Holper
Managing Editor: Anne Uetz
Editorial Assistants

Poetry: Ann Gillidette, Claudia A. Keelan, Mark Muckleroy, George Taylor
Fiction: Mike Clasby, Ron Kuka
Publicity: Radio Station KHSU, Jay Schock
Faculty Advisor: James Galvin
Production Advisor: Jorie Graham
Cover Design: Dar Spain, HSU Media Graphics
Cover Lettering: Jay Brown, HSU Media Graphics
Typesetting: HSU Word Processing
Printing: BUG Press, Arcata

1983
Editor: Dave Holper
Assistant Editor: Jodi Stutz
Editorial Assistants –
Poetry: Norris Beaird, Lori Callies, Nanette Kondrit, Mark Muckleroy, Brenda Todaro
Fiction: Manny Benson, Todd Case, Warren Maher, Pat Millius, Dave Sandars
Faculty Advisor: Judith Minty
Production Manager: Pat Cudahy
Cover Photo: Kathy Vouchilas

1984
Editor: Jodi Stutz
Assistant Editor: Charley Hanley
Editorial Board: Todd Case, Tony Forder, Patricia Forthun, Alan Goodman, Laurel Hoggan, Michele Kagan, Nicholas Karavatos, Theresa Love, Angela Rayburn, Kelly Roach, David Sanders, Jeanne Whitmer
Faculty Advisor: Judith Minty
Production Advisor: Robert Gluckson
Cover Design: Hélene Keter

1985
Editor: Charley Hanley
Poetry Assistant: Nicholas Karavatos
Prose Assistant: David Sanders
Art Assistant: Dan Johnson
Production Assistant: Tony Forder
Co-Editors, 1986: Laurel Tueling, Michele Kagan
Prose Board: Ted Barry, Bruce Black, Charley Hanley, Paul Hoornbeek, Ronna Johnson, Katherine Kalthoff, Matina Kilkenny, Julie Lauer, Chris Neumeyer, David Sanders
Poetry Board: Kevin Cassell, Janet Gary, Pamela Gaynor, Charley Hanley, Dan Johnson, Michelle Kagan, Nicholas Karavatos, Richard Russell, Laurie Simmons, Laurel Tueling
Cover Photo: Doug MacCourt
Cover Design: Dan Johnson
Faculty Advisor: Judith Minty

1986
Co-Editors: Laurel Tueling, Michele Kagan
Assistant Editor: Daryl Chinn
Art Assistants: R.D. Schroyer, Lorna Lundeen-Brown
Production Assistant: Jeff Raby
Prose Board: Warren Hays, Janet Gary, Sharon Waechter,

Tiffany Howard, Leigh Cartwright, Katie Hunter
Poetry Board: Cynthia Gillam Sullivan, Dennis Sullivan, R. Dan Schroyer, Scott Miller, Bruce Black, Leigh Cartwright, Daryl Chinn
Cover: A Graphic Impressions Design by
Lorna Lundeen- Brown
Faculty Advisor: Judith Minty

1987

Editors: Daryl Chinn, Cindy Gillam Sullivan, Dennis Sullivan
Assistant Editors and Editors for Toyon 1988: Scott L. Miller, Sharon Waechter
Fiction Board: Christel Behrens, Leigh Cartwright, Ed Hughes, Michele Kagan, Deborah Lielasus, Scott L. Miller, Sharon Waechter
Poetry Board: Christel Behrens, Gigi Cooper, S. Leanna Harrison, Nicholas Karavatos, Greg Kerstetter, Lisa Pira, Cheryl Seidner, Ann ter Haar, Margaret Wilson, Zanna Vegsundvaag
"Raymond Carver Short Story Contest Board: Jeanne Whitmer (Coordinator), Michael McClure (Assistant Coordinator), Susan Buscher, Roger Cinnamond, Irene Culver, Barry Dal sant, Kevin Fox, Sheila Gallien, Wayne Goellner, Rick Jordan, Cion Maready, Michael Matthews, Diana Murphy, Bob Nelson, Ken Nessel, Kimberly Nightingale, Christopher Nokes, Lisa Pira, Juliane Poirier, Shyla Sickels, Greg Thompson, Jack Turner, Susanne Whitmer"
Faculty Advisor: Judith Minty
Copy Editor:
Ruth Mountaingrove
Cover: A Graphic Impressions Design by Chae Song

1988

Editors: Scott L. Miller, Sharon Waechtor
Fiction Board: Nancy Weitz, Heather D.J. Clark, Linda Aragon, Bob Nelson, Chris Behrens
Poetry Board: Gigi Cooper, Nicholas Karavatos, Vicki Kite, Leanna Harrison, Chris Behrens, Patrick Johnston, Dan Schroyer
"Raymond Carver Short Story Contest Board: Jeanne Whitmer, Michael McClure (Coordinators), Readers: Jim Allen, Linda Bennette, Anoinette Botari, Bob Burroughs, Nancy Calhoun, Bob Chapman, Heather Clark, Becky Emmons, Barbara Hackett, Dee Hawksworth, Jan Joki, Rick Jordan, Michele Kagan, Dave Leslie, Patricia Lyons, Chris Manning, Michael M. Michael, Diana Murphy, Linda O'Roke, Joanne Pieper, Dana Pilarowski, Kathleen Siverson, Joe Stefani,

Sue Whitmer"
Faculty Advisor & Copy Editor: Judith Minty
Cover: Cheryl Ann Coon & University Graphics

1989
Poetry Editor: Steve Hayward
Poetry Board: Linda Aragon, Nancy Calhoun, Mike Michaels, Nancy Short, Loretta Zurth
Fiction Editor: Dave Leslie
Fiction Board: Ann Dziachan, Peter Farley, Eric Fong, John Lutzow, Patricia Lyons, Shelly Mitchel, Charlie Robertson
Editorial Assistant: Dee Hawksworth
Cover "Out the Door" by Valenya

1990
Editors: John Lutzow, Rick Jordan
Assistant Editor: Dee Hawksworth
Editorial Board: Lori Brooks, John Byrnes-Lang, Vince Gotera, Jeff McTear, Heather Morgan, Venetia Rivera, Jason Strange, Brian Waters
Faculty Advisor: Judith Minty
"Raymond Carver Short Story Contest Board: Diana Murphy (Coordinator), Bob Burroughs, Bob Chapman, Barry Dalsant, Gayle Fornataro, Amanda Gray, Vince Gotera, Kim Halliday, Jennifer Hawkins, Dee Hawksworth, Barbara Henry, Thomas Hjerpe, Annette Holland, Marguerite Howell, Melissa Kirk, Erin Lewis, Anna Macbriar, Geneva Miller, Kristin Millich, Clarissa Muzzy, Rosalind Novick, Randy Omersherman, Rachel Orourke, Celeste Pace, Venetia Rivera, Terrence Robinson, Patricia Roller, Robert Schrag, Beth Schroeder, Darlene Seffel, Troy Setterlund, Lynette Spencer, Ronald Stathes, Jack Turner, Eric Vanetten, Geraldine Vinson, Gillian Wegener
Faculty Advisor: Judith Minty

1991
Editors: Jason Strange, Robert Scheer
Assistant Editors: Karen Allendorf, Steven Forrest Peralta
Editorial Board: Lori Brooks, Vincent Cardinale, Anna Hansen Jeffress, Franklin, Celia Homesley, Donna Horton, Lindsey S. Johnson, Ronda Lenci, Dan Levinson, Suzanne Mallett, Jennifer McNally, Heather Morgan, Patrice Reynolds, Lisa Rice, John Rose
Faculty Advisor: Judith Minty
"Raymond Carver Short Story Contest Staff: Patricia Roller (Coordinator), Kim Halliday (Assistant Coordinator), Readers: Robin Ashbaugh, Katie Bakken, Stacy Bliss, Tiffany Boucher, Tricia Boyce, Jennifer Buchanan, Jennifer Buti, Lisa Crummey, Angela Davis, Chris Doane, Kathleen Doty, Alisen Douglas, Laura Feister, John Gladding, Vince Gotera, Terry Gunderson,

Anna Hansen Jeffress, Debra Hartridge, Sally Jager, Katie Jonas, Jennifer Klaffke, Kim Lekas, Erin Lewis, Christina Lexutt, Suzanne Mallett, Roy McKenna, Dick McPherson, Heather Morgan, Kim Myers, Michelle Paloutzian, Jeff Paris, Kate Peltier, Desiree Pritchard, Alex Quici, Tracey Rembert, John Rose, Paul Runnells, Rebecca Schuett, Tiffany Schultz, Joe Stefani, Darcy Stockton, Ronda Stritzel, Deborah Sultan, Darcy Wandler, Stacy Waymire, Johnnie Wilcox, Nicole Zeller"
Faculty Advisor: Judith Minty

1992

Editors: Karen Allendorf, Steven Forrest Peralta
Assistant Editors: Penny Jahnke Tarpey, Michael Boren
Reading Staff: Deborah Addington, Bradford Barry, Gregory Carter, Jodi Henderson, Kimberly Miller, Paul Miller, Brett Newland, Ana Otero, Laura Paselk, Alexander Quici, Kristen Schuster, Elisa Sedam, Karen Sylvest, Michael Turner, Richard Vanderkam, Brett Wilsey, Theresa Wilson
Faculty Advisor: Judith Minty
"Raymond Carver Short Story Contest Staff: Randy Omer-Sherman (Coordinator), Jeffrey Paris (Assistant Coordinator), Readers: Randy Accetta, Deborah Addington, Angelee Allen, Chela Anderson, Robin Ashbaugh, Gina Bottino, David Cochran, Michelle Contreras, Marc Costanza, Alexander D'Arcy, Joshua Daughdrill, Joseph Ferreira, Rebecca Gilbert, Paul Grafton, Juliana Haverluck, Mark Hayward, Marguerite Howell, Ann Ingraham, Marjorie Jackson, Trisha Johnston, John Kalinowski, Mary Keegan, Eytan Klawer, Erin Lewis, Sarah McCaughey, Terrance McNally II, Mathew McPhee, Jennifer Medina, Karen Montaguereyes, Jeffrey Nelson, Lan Nguyen, Karlyn Pleasants, Jacob Powell, Jennifer Proenza, Alexander Quici, Tera Reeve, Tracey Rembert, Wilfredo Reyes, Stephanie Robbins, Curtis Sanford, Elisa Sedam, Alicia Sitz, Katrina Smith, Richard Smith, Daniel Stead, Joanne Straley, Jennifer Todd, Kevin Tolley, Jolie Uritz, Melissa Van Gelderen, Gary Weaver, Michael Woods, Carmen Ybarra"
Faculty Advisor: Judith Minty

1993

Editors: Michael Boren, Penny Jahnke Tarpey
Assistant Editors: Celia Homesley, Brett Newland, Elissa Fisher
Reading Staff: Donna Bankson, Laura Boyd, Colleen Cadwallader, Ruth Canaway, Tracy Carlson, Margaret Cashion, Kimberly Childers, Christopher Cooper, Abigail

Dean, Sonia Espinoza, Susan Mumm Fitzgerald, Taunya Funston, Josh Goldfaden, Michelle Green, Gina Hassel, Mark Hendricks, Gina Hill, Ann Ingraham, David Liles, Roy Mckenna, Ruth Mountaingrove, James Olson, Lisa Rice, Karen Romani, Louis Springer, Daniel Stead, Sylvia Stephens, Stephen Warren, Blake Weathers

Cover Art: Michael Boren

Faculty Advisor: Judith Minty

"Raymond Carver Short Story Contest Staff: Kim Halliday (Coordinator), Laurie Mikulasek (Assistant Coordinator), Readers: Michael Ady, Karen Anderson, Aileen Arbaugh, Elizabeth Barnes, Jessica Bennett, Patricia Biteman, Laura Boyd, Tracy Carlson, Michelle Contreras, Marc Costanza, Jennifer Davis, Wendy Day, John Digiacinto, Kristina Dinkelbach, Laura Dring, Amy Ferreira, Taunya Funston, Crystal Gardner, Kathleen Garvey, Michelle Green, Mark Grondona, Pamela Hale, Alison Hanna, Brandi Hyson, Anne Ingraham, John Kirby, Nancy Knowles, Debra Linhares, Lonnie Lopez, Terry Lopez, Ruth Mountaingrove, Eric Nyman, Doreen Orindo, Brian Padian, Lisa Rice, Karen Romani, Timothy Roth, Jesse Saich, Abigail Samoun, Timothy Schneider, Kristen Schuster, Sean Seidell, Peri Smith, Jennifer Tatkin, Traci Treffert, Blake Weathers, Jamie White, Kristen York"

Faculty Advisor: Judith Minty

1994

Editors: Elissa Fisher, Celia Homesley

Associate Editor/Copy Editor: Ann King Ingraham

Reading Staff: Michael Barba, Michael Boren, Kim Cabrera, Colleen Cadwallader, Christopher Cooper, Paul Grafton, Nancy Karraker, Brad Kerstetter, Bill McLellan, Paul Miller, Jennifer Moline, Mary Carol Skordy, Penney Tarpey

Faculty Advisor: Vince Gotera

"Raymond Carver Short Story Contest Staff: Kim Halliday, Laurie Mikulasek (Coordinators), Reading Staff: Elizabeth Bearden, Genevieve Berquist, Lorraine Breer, Amandy Browning, Kim Cabrera, Pamela Chateauneuf, Kampol Crews, Lisa Cunningham, Stacey Doering, Brandy Flores, Brian Forsyth, Jennifer Forsyth, Josh Goldfaden, Jennifer Gow, Nicole Hales, Holly Hamilton, Lisa Hernandez, Katherine Kirkham, Emily Lahr, Tara Lawrence, Kristi Leal, Michelle Mercer, Abraham Meyer, Marla Netzer, Ana O, Kimberly Parsons, Alisa Pelanconi, Cari Pogan, Tracy Rembert, Ivan Rosenburg, Carrie Russell, Esther Scannell, David Stier, John Tarvin IV, Kimberly

White, Deidre Wibberley, Richard Williams, Wendy Zimmer"
Faculty Advisor: Vince Gotera

1995
Managing Editor: Christopher Cooper
Poetry & Production Editor: eytan klawer
Fiction Editor: Matthew Nicely
Art Editor: Lara Wells
Readers: Rachel Aldrich, Maria-Daniel Asturias, Jennifer Black, Michael Bresnahan, Lori Brooks, Kim Cabrera, Christina Coussens, Teagan Decker, Kristie Fogg, Ryan Gerhardt, Kevin Harvey, Deborah Henry, Sean McAuley, Terrance McNally, Jennifer Moline, Samuel Nord, Ronald Renspie, Ann Rohde, Robert Romano, Taylor Schuss, Michael Schwartz, Leuckessia Spencer, John Tarvin, Brandon Totman, Cherlyn Wisdom, Tammy Wittler, Merrold Young
Faculty Advisor: Vince Gotera
"Raymond Carver Short Story Staff: Marla Netzer (Co-coordinator), Christopher Olson (Co-coordinator), Reading Staff: Aimee Adams, Deborah Addington, Shoshanna Ariss, Jennifer Black, Tempra Board, Amy Brackett, Valerie Brandtjen, Judith Breece, Lorraine Breer, Kimberly Cabrera, Tamra Claus, Adam Conley, Natalie Cull, Lynn Davis, Brian Derr, Tara Dolan, Joe Erven, Sun Ezzell, Terry Hall, Deborah Henry, Marcy Henzel, Dawn Holt, Dorte Jensen, Karin Kelley, Ljubica Knezevich, Sophie Lawrence, Daniel Lee, Jason Leibert, Kari Mann, Andrea Chevoya, Lisa Mugavero, Maria Netzer, Eva Paterson, Jon Patmore, Dolores Perez, Tina Perry, James Peterson, Brandi Price, Ronald Racillis, Karen Richardson, Ann Rohde, Chelsea Ross, Hannah Rossoff, Jessica Savage, Melissa Schmidt, Elisabeth Schneider, William Stellin, Sylvia Stephens, Kristina Thewlis, Nydia Torres, John Velasquez, April Watson, Derek Willard, Timaree Marston, Lindsay Mathews, Mason Matteoil, Sean McAuley, Heidi Mermis-Cava, Terra Caldwell, Kimberly Clarke
Faculty Advisor: Vince Gotera
Judge: Judith Minty

1996
Fiction Editor: Mike Wilcutt
Poetry Editor: Kari Mann
Art Director/Production Manager: Christina Begley
Calyx Anais, Terra Caldwell, Erin Duke, Tyler Dunivant, Dwight Glennon, Ryan Graham, Robin Hales, Errin Haskins, Greg Hoetker, Lisa Hoffman, Greg Holder, Natasha Hudson, Jennifer Large, Heather Lawson, Megan Marshall, Allen Maxwell, Tamara Nelson, Allison Pasto,

Jim Peterson, David Spain, Shannon Stuart, Tyler Vack, Kristy Wright, Elizabeth Zdunich
"Short Story Contest: Dorte Jensen, Amandy Browning (Co-coordinators), Heather Angier, Abhishek Bajpal, Amy Baugh-Meyer, Amalla Beard, Elizabeth Bearden, Jean Belef, Jennifer Black, Amandy Browning, Maryn Burnley, Stacy Campbell, Sunshine Caufield, Kory Christenson, Adam Church, Amanda Covey, Carol Croissant, Erin DeMars, Shannon Fink, Richard Garcia, Matthew Goldsworthy, Jennifer Gow, Wendy Grear, Damara Hall, Ryan Harris, Charles Hoey, Sayaka Ito, Jennifer Jenkins, Dorte Jensen, Dennis Johnson, Jennifer King, Jeanne Konljn, Marie Laurey, Corrie Littlejohn, Jason Luke, Andres Marin, Benjamin Marshall, Timaree Marston, William McCloskey, Cheryl Mietz, Raphael Mischel, Jenice Mize, Arlana Moise, Randall Morris, Coralysa Murphy, Jennifer Naumann, Sandra Nine, Shoshana Paster, Daniel Perry, Jeffery Pollard, James Rasmussen, Michelle Ridlehoover, Dianne Sigman, David Spain, Jason Strengren, Christopher Sweet, Nydle Torres, Thomas Valterria, Michelle Waliar, Adena West, Robert Wilson, Dorian Wright, Kristy Wright, Elan Young, Priscilla Zelada"
Judge: Vince Gotera
Advisor: Dan Levinson

1998
Fiction Editor: David M. Spain
Poetry Editor: Jennifer Large
Art Editor: Katherine Almy
Assistant Editor: Andrea Gyurancsik
Faculty Advisor: Jim Dodge
Raymond Carver Short Story: Lorraine A. Michaels (Contest Coordinator), Melanie Jackson (Judge)
Readers: Erik Betzschmidt, Laura Boyd, Heather Buck, Amy Crowley, Jennifer Cruz, Elizabeth Escutia, Laura Friudenberg, Matt Garland, Forrest Gillespie, Bernadette Johnson, Gillian Nadler, Tanja Notkoff, Mark Owens, Anna Reinholz, Sandra Remick, Anne Rohde, Jon Schneider, Andra Schreiber, Joi Young

1999
Coordinating Editor: Tanja Notkoff
Fiction Editor: Forrest Gillespie
Art & Layout Editor: David B. Lee
Poetry Editor: Peter Perata
Assistant Art Editor: Kevin Boyle
Faculty Advisor: Jim Dodge
"Raymond Carver Short Story Contest: Lorraine Michaels (Contest Coordinator), Richard Cortez Day (Judge), *Toyon* Readers: Julia Bernbaum,

Tim Bowden, Marc Carlson, Lisa Connell, Greta Dodson, James Faulk, Andrea Gyuranesik, Carlos Harry, Gabe Kelly, Sarah Konshak, Timaree Marston, Hank Nicol, Tim O'Brien, Tamara Rivera, Andra Schreiber, Khristina Walsh"

2000

Coordinating Editor: Peter Perata
Fiction Editor: Sarah Konshak
Poetry Editor: James Faulk
Art and Layout Editor: Kevin Boyle
Assistant Editor: Tim O'Brien
Faculty Advisor: Jim Dodge
Raymond Carver Short Story Contest: Lorraine A. Michaels (Contest Coordinator)
Toyon Readers: Tamara Rivera, Cathi Metz, Rachel Jacobs, Brian Derr, Patrick K. Schulze, Manja Argue-Hoggard, Tamera Britton, Kellii Schurb, Kathryn Leezer, Sharon Freed, Erin Fairchild, Jackie Danelski, Charles Wickman"

2001

Coordinating Editor: Erin Fairchild
Fiction Editor: Sarah Konshak
Poetry Editor: Tamara Britton
Art and Layout Editor: Patrick Schulze
Faculty Advisor: Jim Dodge
Raymond Carver Short Story Contest: Kim Eubanks (Contest Coordinator)
Toyon Readers: John Aceves, Gina Blinkley-Swartz, Jessica Binney, Paige Bohart, Mary Boley, Angela Cheung, Robert Collins, Elizabeth Escutia, Joshua Estavillo, Kyle Giocomo, Rebecca Holland, Kathryn Leezer, Douglas Magnuson, Kelly McNicholas, Julie Neilson, Christina Pirruccello, Catherine Schulze, Damian Taggart, Melanie Traver, Jonathan Turney"

2002

Coordinating Editor: Patrick K. Schulze
Fiction Editor: Stacy Hoffinger
Poetry Editor: Brian Derr
Art and Layout Editor: Lori Brannigan
Faculty Advisor: Jim Dodge
Raymond Carver Short Story Contest: Kim Eubanks (Contest Coordinator)
Toyon Readers: Jeanine Becker, Adele Cameron, Lori Conkling, Scott Cresswell, Beth Deaton, Cristina DeLodder, Jozef deVries, Olympia Franklin, Katie Frey, Katherine McAbee, Allison Miller, Marisa Mosqueda, Andrea Schriner, Linda Smith, Maryann Wood and Chris Wright
Cover photograph: "Touch 1," by Zennin Hilldoor
Back Cover: "Dreams," by Andrew Daniel

2003

Coordinating Editor: Linda L. Smith
Fiction Editor: Mike Swanson
Poetry Editor: Jozef DeVries
Creative Nonfiction Editor: Adam MacDougal
Art and Layout Editor: Linda L. Smith
Faculty Advisor: Jim Dodge
Raymond Carver Short Story Contest: Brian Derr (Contest Coordinator),
Toyon Readers: Jodie Burgess, Margaret Calstrom, Scott Cresswell, Jozef DeVries, Adam MacDougal, Jenny Moffitt, Mike Swanson, Jessamyn West, Richard Wilder, Katie Wilson and Tierra Hodge"

2004

Coordinating Editor: Linda L. Smith
Fiction Editor: Carissa Creel
Assistant Fiction Editor: Jeff Skehen
Poetry Editor: Katie Wilson
Assistant Poetry Editor: Scott Cresswell
Nonfiction Editor: Adam MacDougal
Assistant Nonfiction Editor: Gregory Zobel
Art Editor: Nathaniel Lloyd
Layout Editor: Thavisak Syphanthong
"*Toyon* Readers: Yeshe Azevedo, Brad Bisio, Meghan Dill, Matthew Eckert, Kena Marie Foster, Diana Gonfiotti, Mellisa Hannum, Christina Lease, Natalie Lopez, Holly Mac Donell, Cathi Metz, William Morris, Codee Radford, Cory Ratzlaff, Jessamyn Webb

2005

Coordinating Editor: Carissa Crockenberg
Layout Editor: Tyler J. Hill
Assistant Layout Editor: Dianna Gonfiotti
Poetry Editor: Yeshe Azevedo
Assistant Poetry Editor: Elizabeth Bauer
Fiction Editor: William Morris
Assistant Fiction Editor: Tyler J. Hill
Nonfiction Editor: Melanie Traver
Assistant Nonfiction Editor: Nicole Montee
Art Editor: Jason Smith
Assistant Art Editors: Leah Jorgensen, Nikki Hodgson
Toyon Readers: Yvonne Becker, Chris Blush, Jennifer Bisio, Mary Dunn, Gary Flesher, Manuel Fonseca, Nikki Hodgson, Johanna Jackson, Ken Jarrett, Leah Jorgensen, Kim Kayano, Merrick McKinlay, Ryan Keller, Jacob Kirk, Kai Lillie, Jason Smith, Katie Wilson, Stephanie Yantzer"
Art Reviewers: Kena Marie Foster, Jacob Kirk, Kai Lillie, Merrick McKinlay, Nicole Montee, Stephanie Yantzer
Academic Advisor: Linda L. Smith
Raymond Carver Short Story Contest: Karynn Merkel

2006

Advisor: Jim Dodge
Art Editor: Carolyn Warren
Creative Nonfiction Editor: Kelly Curtis
Fiction Editor: Sarah Holmsen
Poetry Editor: Meghan Dill
Production Editor: Megan Kramer
Production Team: Kelly Curtis, Sarah Holsmen
"Readers: Joe Baker, Tamara Berger, Tasia Block, Nicole Bondurant, Anna Calabrese, Emily Creighton, Kelly Curtis, Meghan Dill, Josh Engle, Devin Farren, Jennifer Hale, Christopher Hall, Jenny Henrikson, Christel Henson, Sarah Holmsen, Alice Knudsen, Megan Kramer, Thor Matuschka, Gary McClough, Nola Pierce, John Post, Bryan Radzin, Brooke Raven, Mary Renslow, Virginia Rolla, Vann Smith, Michelle Song, Kenneth Tejada, Eric Van Note, Stephanie Van Streefkerk, Genevieve Walker, Carolyn Warren"

2007

Cooperative Editors: Drew Allen, Maxfield Atturio, Joe Baker, Jean Belef-Hoggard, Dave Brooksher, Nathan Campbell, Cristina Chohlis, Lauren Connolly, Dustin Crane, Daniel Duffy, Katherine Herr, Erin Kirwan, Philip Kumsar, Patrick Lynch, Naomi Millette, Robert Monteiith, Natasha Newman, Sarah O'Leary, Jessica Osborne, Evelyn Schmelling
Faculty Advisor: Jim Dodge

2008

Cooperative Editors: Bart Baily, Samantha Bettinger, Noelle Brady, Sarah Daum, A. Dominic Efferson, Chris Escarcega, Matt Jackson, Hilal Jamal, Arnold King, Phil Kumsar, Natalie Landreneaux, Elan May, Jen McCollum, Ave Messer, Nathaniel Ochoa, Anthony Pulliam, Erica Scott, Molly Sexton, Brent Smith, Jacob Tucker, Dionne Wasington
Faculty Advisor: Jim Dodge

2009

Posters & Publicity: Perry Cage, Anthony Pulliam
Submission Management: Bev Steichen, Brian Graham, George Walker, William Morris
Poetry Reading Board: Brian Graham
Creative Nonfiction Reading Board: Gayle Healy, Julia Reynolds, Elan May
Fiction Reading Board: William Morris
Art Board: Jake Payne
Copyediting: Elan May, Julia Reynolds
Production: Elan May, Julia Reynolds, Jacob Lehman
Faculty Advisor: Jim Dodge
Cooperative Editors: Bart Bailey, Robert Brewster, Perry Cage, Matt Clementz, Sarah Daily, Joseph Davisson, Brian

Graham, Gayle Healy, Galen Latsko, Gabriel LeDoux, Jacob Lehman, Elan May, William Morris, Jake Payne, Anthony Pulliam, Julia Reynolds, Eileen Russell, Karly Scaletti, Beverley Steichen, Keith Tulley, Leah Valdivia, George Walker

2010
Managing Editor: Julia Reynolds
Poetry Editor: Julianna Bagwell
Fiction Editor: Melissa Waldman
Art Editor: Briana Contreras
Non Fiction Editors: Mackenzie Cox and Evan Curry
Layout Editors: Shelby Chandler, Leslie Meyer, and Emily Roles
Editorial Staff: Stephen Adams, Jonathan Barrett, Perry Cage, Sylvia Evridge, Jennifer Frankhauser, Morgan Ferris, John Hill, Tina Kumar, Rebecca Martin, Ashlee Murieta, Brittany Osterhout, Alexis Pereira, Coral Pope, Jacob Pounds, Arren Propster Ben Ramey, Isain Reyes, Kenka Rodgers, Katherine White, Tracy Yabiku

2011
Coordinating Editor: Shalyn Eppler
Poetry Editor: Laurel Jean
Fiction Editor: Robert Gerleman
Creative Nonfiction Editor: Phillip Schatz
Art Editor: Abbey Touchette
Layout Editor: Chris Hancock, Jonathan Barrett, Samuel Bryant, Ian Carter, Natalie Chagollan, Jacqueline Colla Anthony Correale, Travis Fortenberry, Sarah Harter, Michael Jay, Daniel Ogulu, Amber Okeh, Chelsea Slevin, Nicholas Smillie, Phoebe Smith, Nicole Spencer Ronna Wareh
Kyle Windhem
Yiling Yan

Faculty Advisor: Corey Lewis
Teaching Assistant: Julia Reynolds

2012
Managing Editor: Robert Gerleman
Poetry Editor: Andrew Garai
Fiction Editor: Guthrie L'Herogan
Creative Nonfiction Editor: Julieanne Hope
Art Editor: Abbey Touchette
Layout Editor: Shalyn Eppler
Editorial Staff: Chelsea Barber, Daarian Bringle, Tess Cervantes, Christian Chenault, Jacqueline Colla, Leigha Evers, Theresa Goldstein, Krista Isaksen, Matt Koker, Becca Kramer, Kayla Molander, Yajaira Padilla, Lauren Pang, Michael Ray Menjivar, Ashlyn Rhodes, Phillip Schatz, Chelsea Slevin, Nick Smillie, Leticia Snoots, Jen Thornberg, Shaina Varble-Paladino, Ashley Ward
Faculty Advisor: Dr. Corey Lewis

Past Toyon Staff

Teaching Assistant:
Shalyn Eppler

2013
Managing Editors: Azuree D. Lovely-Ramsey and Tess C. Wilder-Cervantes
Division Editors
Fiction: Thomas Oliver
Poetry: Michael Ray Menjivar
Creative Nonfiction: Frederic Randall III
Art: Kristine Avila
Literary Criticism: Dr. Corey Lewis
Editorial Staff, Fiction and Creative Nonfiction: Stephannie Arcadia, Kylie Bay, Terence Brierly, Christian Chenault, Leigha Evers, Erin Galloway, Kevin Gullufsen, Hannah Hunter, Jorina Laurin, Jamie Lembeck
Editorial Staff, Poetry and Art: Tori Asato, Timothy Bliss, Evan Curry, Trae Garza, Kyle Hinshaw, Matthew Koker, Ethan Naszady, Jacquelyn Robinson

Faculty Advisor:
Dr. Corey Lewis

2014
Managing Editors: Kyle Hinshaw, Terence Brierly, Thomas Oliver
Division Editors:
Art: Hayden Newman
Creative Nonfiction: Elizabeth Powers
Fiction: Kylie Bay
Poetry: John Papadopoulos and Christopher Wilkie
Editorial Staff Readers, Creative Nonfiction and Fiction: Michael Estrada, Amanda Brunell, Claire Unruh, Ashley Underwood, Kirsten Collins, Kenneth Rainey

Editorial Staff Readers, Poetry and Art: Annie Brownwood, Abbey Byers, Danny Chavez, Wyatt Reno
Faculty Advisor:
Dr. Corey Lewis

2015
Managing Editors: Terence Brierly and Clayton Ellis
Division Editor, Art: Maia Cheli-Colando
Division Editor, Creative Non-Fiction: Ashley Underwood
Division Editor, Fiction: Stephanie Cargill-Greer
Division Editor, Poetry: Thomas King
Editorial Staff Readers: James Cookman, Mario Cortez. Amethyst Forrest. Renee Gurule, Darren Nuzzo. Katie Oxley, Michelle. Christopher Wyart
Faculty Advisor:
Dr. Laurie A. Pinkert

2016
Managing Editors: Clayton Ellis and Angela Compton
Copyeditor: A.J. McGough
Acquisitions Editor: Michael Robinson
Creative Nonfiction Editor: Jasmin Arnold
Poetry Editors: Bri Lucero and

Jocelyn Aguilar
Fiction Editors: Clarissa Call and A.J. McGough
Translation and Multilingual Editor: Andrea Curtade
Visual Art Editor: Dane Manary
Special Theme Editor: Luke Wages
Spoken Word & Audio Editor: Rose Christy-Cirillo
Web Manager: Gabe Pacana
Archive Editor: Jade Mejia
Circulation Manager: Nils Rabe
Events Coordinators: Ryan Silva and Marin Hilger
Social Media Manager: Marley Coody
Office Manager: Amy Whitney
Internal Communications Manager: Elena Kay
Faculty Advisor: Janelle Adsit

2017
Managing Editor: Angela Compton
Assistant Managing Editor: Sydney Hubbel
Internal Communications Manager: Kelley Ellion
Archive Editor: AJ McGough
Social Media Manager: Ciera Townsley-McCormick
Writers' and Artists' Communities Liaison: Amanda Walker
Print and Radio Media Liaison: Jackie Lowe
Translation Editor: Jan Calderon
Acquisitions Editor & Copyeditors: Jocelyn Aguilar & Bri Lucero
Multilingual Editor: Grant Rowley
Poetry Editors: Ángela Ibarra & Anastasia Rivera
Creative NonFiction Editors: Grace Hart & Lydia Leonard-Rhodes
Fiction Editors: Marina Fittinghoff & Maddy Kopsick
Environmental Justice Editors: Shiloh Green & Miranda Olberg
Literary Criticism Editors: Kelley Ellion & Sydney Hubbel
Spoken Word and Audio Editor: Brooke Minner
Visual Art Editors: Jared Amerman, Jesi Hamilton, & Gabby Szmidt
Production Editor, Typesetter, & Proofreader: Claudia Jimenez
Events Coordinator: Jessica Stiles
Faculty Advisor: Janelle Adsit

2018
Managing Editor: Kelley Ellion
Multilingual Editors: Christina Molina Ceja and Tania Trinidad
Poetry Editors: Hunter Thom and Grace Hart
Creative Non Fiction Editor: Laura Thompson
Fiction Editors: Madison Reed-Stacy and Wyatt Georgeson
Environmental Justice Editors: Kendra Gardner and Mattie Salinas
Literary Criticism Editor:

Hallie Lepphaille
Spoken Word Editors: Erin Scofield, Joel Segura, and Liliana Del Rio
Visual Arts Editors: Cheyanne Seely and Nicholas Graham
Outreach Team: Anthony Alonzo-Pereira, Literary Translator; Aly Smith, Social Media Manager; Nicholas Graham, Communities Liaison; Megan Lombardo, Media Liaison; Korinza Shlanta, Archive Editor; Audrey DiGenova, Circulation Manager
Production Team: Christopher Bailey, Proofreader; Sydney Hubbel, Typesetter
Additional Proofreaders: Brian Arriola, Liliana Del Rio, Sarah Godlin, Bryan Kashon, Harry Liddic, Citlally Moreno Gomez, Mireille Roman, Joel Segura, Carter Solomon, Kayla Stark, Destiny Wright
Faculty Advisor: Janelle Adsit

2019
Managing Editor: Anthony Alonzo-Pereira
Assistant Managing Editor: Erika Andrews
Secretary: Salina Jimenez
Treasurer: Destiny Wright
Social Media Managers: Madeline Bauman and Kayla Stark
Literary and Artist Community Liaison: Asha Galindo
Editorial Team Lead / Acquisitions Editors: Ashley Alvarez and Mireille Roman
Division Editors, Critical Analysis: Gloria Pearlman-Warren and Zach Weaver
Division Editors, Creative Nonfiction: Liliana Del Rio and Jasmine Nazario
Division Editors, Fiction: Drew Ahlberg and Joel Segura
Division Editors, Poetry: Theressa Lopez and Heather Rumsey
Spoken Word / Web Team Lead: Erika Andrews
Division Editors, Spoken Word: Deanna Abate, Quinn Dobbins, and Dean Engle
Archive Editor: Hannah Hoskisson
Production Team Leads: Sarah Godlin and Carter Solomon
Visual Art Editor: Noelle Peterson
Typesetter: Max Hosford
Book Designers: Sarah Godlin and Carter Solomon
Audiobook Director: Dean Engle
Faculty Advisor: Janelle Adsit

2020
Managing Editor: Erika Andrews
Assistant Managing Editor & Community Liaison: Theressa Lopez
Editorial Team Leads / Acquisitions Editors: Alec Cox and Alice Jiang
Division Editors, Fiction and Playwriting: Alexandria Weber and Alexis Avitia
Division Editors, Creative Nonfiction: Jessica Lewis and

Danielle Dornan
Division Editors, Poetry: Keith Gonsalves and Megan Graeser
Division Editors, Literary Criticism: Alexis Avitia and Maximilian J Heirich
Team Lead & Social Media Manager: Sam Dunlap
Spoken Word Editors: Cahner Cameron-D'Angelo and Todd Loughran
Archive Editor: Mary Lipiec
Division Editor for the Environmental Justice Award: Sam Dunlap
Production Team Leads & Multilingual Proofreaders: Drew Ahlberg and Milagros Ortega
Visual Art Editors and Cover Designers: Kayla Riley and Rae Diamond
Typesetters and Book Designers: Paweenaporn Pongampornsakda and Helen Berry
Division Editors for the Multilingual Award: Milagros Ortega and Paweenaporn Pongampornsakda
Audiobook Narrators: Tim Arceneaux, Helen Berry, Zoey Buitrago, Jennifer Dabbs, Rae Diamond, Keith Gonzalves, Will Hamann, Theressa Lopez, Alice Jiang, Todd Loughran Rachel Matteri, Brea Pratt, Imari Washington, Selena Weltz
Audiobook Director: Cahner Cameron D'Angelo
Ebook Designers: Drew Ahlberg, Jessica Lewis, Rachel Matteri, Brea Pratt
Faculty Advisor: Janelle Adsit
Toyon Administrator: Marcos Hernandez

2021

Translation Team: Natalie Raquel Acuña, Ernie Iniguez, Brittany Muñoz-Garcia
Production Team: Joshua Lamason, Rhett Davis, Heidi Woods
Publicity Team: Junee Banks, Alison Silver, Aria Lentini
Ebook Team: Sheryl Colgrove, Rachel O'Shaughnessy
Audiobook and Spoken Word Team:
Connie Pearson, Alex Weber, Sloan Volenec

www.ingramcontent.com/pod-product-compliance
Lightning Source LLC
Chambersburg PA
CBHW050750110526
44592CB00002B/21